Annika

6th Grade

Advisor

Mike L

Level 1

¡Avancemos!

Unit 3 Resource Book

McDougal Littell
A DIVISION OF HOUGHTON MIFFLIN COMPANY
Evanston, Illinois • Boston • Dallas

*AP and the Advanced Placement Program are registered trademarks of the College Entrance
Examination Board, which was not involved in the production of and does not endorse this product.

Fine Art Acknowledgements

Page 86 *La Plaza de Colón* (1986), Manuel Hernández Acevedo. Oil on board. Collection of Arte de
la Cooperativa de Seguros Múltiples, San Juan, Puerto Rico. © 2005 Víctor Manuel Hernández/
Estate of Manuel Hernández Acevedo.

Page 87 *Cantor criollo* (1962), Augusto Marín. Oil on masonite, 48"x 44". Collection of Arte
de la Cooperativa Seguros Múltiples, San Juan, Puerto Rico. Courtesy of Lisi Marín, San Juan,
Puerto Rico.

Page 88 *Goyita* (1949), Rafael Tufiño. Oil on canvas, 25 1/2" x 21". Photograph by John
Betancourt. Courtesy of Pablo Tufiño.

Page 89 *José Campeche at the Door to Old San Juan* (1976), Lorenzo Homar. Screen print.
Graphic Arts Collection. Department of Rare Books and Special Collections. Princeton University/
Courtesy of the Homar Family.

ISBN-13: 978-0-618-76614-7
ISBN-10: 0-618-76614-6

7 8 9 10 1431   17 16 15
4500533394

McDougal Littell

¡Avancemos!

Table of Contents

To the Teacher

Welcome to *¡Avancemos!* This exciting new Spanish program from McDougal Littell has been designed to provide you—the teacher of today's foreign language classroom—with comprehensive pedagogical support.

PRACTICE WITH A PURPOSE

Activities throughout the program begin by establishing clear goals. Look for the **¡Avanza!** arrow that uses student-friendly language to lead the way towards achievable goals. Built-in self-checks in the student text (**Para y piensa:** Did you get it?) offer the chance to assess student progress throughout the lesson. Both the student text and the workbooks offer abundant leveled practice to match varied student needs.

CULTURE AS A CORNERSTONE

¡Avancemos! celebrates the cultural diversity of the Spanish-speaking world by motivating students to think about similarities and contrasts among different Spanish-speaking cultures. Essential questions encourage thoughtful discussion and comparison between different cultures.

LANGUAGE LEARNING THAT LASTS

The program presents topics in manageable chunks that students will be able to retain and recall. "Recycle" topics are presented frequently so students don't forget material from previous lessons. Previously learned content is built upon and reinforced across the different levels of the program.

TIME-SAVING TEACHER TOOLS

Simplify your planning with McDougal Littell's exclusive teacher resources: the all-inclusive EasyPlanner DVD-ROM, ready-made Power Presentations, and the McDougal Littell Assessment System.

Unit Resource Book

Each Unit Resource Book supports a unit of *¡Avancemos!* The Unit Resource Books provide a wide variety of materials to support, practice, and expand on the material in the *¡Avancemos!* student text.

Components **Following is a list of components included in each Unit Resource Book:**

BACK TO SCHOOL RESOURCES (UNIT 1 ONLY)

Review and start-up activities to support the **Lección preliminar** of the textbook.

DID YOU GET IT? RETEACHING & PRACTICE COPYMASTERS

 If students' performance on the **Para y piensa** self-check for a section does not meet your expectations, consider assigning the corresponding Did You Get It? Reteaching and Practice Copymasters. These copymasters provide extensive reteaching and additional practice for every vocabulary and grammar presentation section in *¡Avancemos!* Each vocabulary and grammar section has a corresponding three-page copymaster. The first page of the copymaster reteaches the subject material in a fresh manner. Immediately following this presentation page are two pages of practice exercises that help the student master the topic. The practice pages have engaging contexts and structures to retain students' attention.

PRACTICE GAMES

These games provide fun practice of the vocabulary and grammar just taught. They are targeted in scope so that each game practices a specific area of the **lesson**: *Práctica de vocabulario*, *Vocabulario en contexto*, *Práctica de gramática*, *Gramática en contexto*, *Todo junto*, *Repaso de la lección*, and the lesson's cultural information.

Video and audio resources

VIDEO ACTIVITIES

These two-page copymasters accompany the Vocabulary Video and each scene of the **Telehistoria** in Levels 1 and 2 and the **Gran desafío** in Level 3. The pre-viewing activity asks students to activate prior knowledge about a theme or subject related to the scene they will watch. The viewing activity is a simple activity for students to complete as they watch the video. The post-viewing activity gives students the opportunity to demonstrate comprehension of the video episode.

VIDEO SCRIPTS

This section provides the scripts of each video feature in the unit.

AUDIO SCRIPTS

This section contains scripts for all presentations and activities that have accompanying audio in the student text as well as in the two workbooks (*Cuaderno: práctica por niveles* and *Cuaderno para hispanohablantes*) and the assessment program.

Culture resources

MAP/CULTURE ACTIVITIES

This section contains a copymaster with geography and culture activities based on the Unit Opener in the textbook.

FINE ART ACTIVITIES

The fine art activities in every lesson ask students to analyze pieces of art that have been selected as representative of the unit location country. These copymasters can be used in conjunction with the full-color fine art transparencies in the Unit Transparency Book.

Home-school connection

FAMILY LETTERS & FAMILY INVOLVEMENT ACTIVITIES

This section is designed to help increase family support of the students' study of Spanish. The family letter keeps families abreast of the class's progress, while the family involvement activities let students share their Spanish language skills with their families in the context of a game or fun activity.

ABSENT STUDENT COPYMASTERS

The Absent Student Copymasters enable students who miss part of a **lesson** to go over the material on their own. The checkbox format allows teachers to choose and indicate exactly what material the student should complete. The Absent Student Copymasters also offer strategies and techniques to help students understand new or challenging information.

Core Ancillaries in the ¡Avancemos! Program

Leveled workbooks

CUADERNO: PRÁCTICA POR NIVELES

This core ancillary is a leveled practice workbook to supplement the student text. It is designed for use in the classroom or as homework. Students who can complete the activities correctly should be able to pass the quizzes and tests. Practice is organized into three levels of difficulty, labeled A, B, and C. Level B activities are designed to practice vocabulary, grammar, and other core concepts at a level appropriate to most of your students. Students who require more structure can complete Level A activities, while students needing more of a challenge should be encouraged to complete the activities in Level C. Each level provides a different degree of linguistic support, yet requires students to know and handle the same vocabulary and grammar content.

The following sections are included in *Cuaderno: práctica por niveles* for each **lesson**:

Vocabulario A, B, C	Escuchar A, B, C
Gramática 1 A, B, C	Leer A, B, C
Gramática 2 A, B, C	Escribir A, B, C
Integración: Hablar	Cultura A, B, C
Integración: Escribir	

CUADERNO PARA HISPANOHABLANTES

This core ancillary provides leveled practice for heritage learners of Spanish. Level A is for heritage learners who hear Spanish at home but who may speak little Spanish themselves. Level B is for those who speak some Spanish but don't read or write it yet and who may lack formal education in Spanish. Level C is for heritage learners who have had some formal schooling in Spanish. These learners can read and speak Spanish, but may need further development of their writing skills. The *Cuaderno para hispanohablantes* will ensure that heritage learners practice the same basic grammar, reading, and writing skills taught in the student text. At the same time, it offers additional instruction and challenging practice designed specifically for students with prior knowledge of Spanish.

The following sections are included in *Cuaderno para hispanohablantes* for each **lesson**:

Vocabulario A, B, C	Integración: Hablar
Vocabulario adicional	Integración: Escribir
Gramática 1 A, B, C	Lectura A, B, C
Gramática 2 A, B, C	Escritura A, B, C
Gramática adicional	Cultura A, B, C

Other Ancillaries

ASSESSMENT PROGRAM

For each level of *¡Avancemos!*, there are four complete assessment options. Every option assesses students' ability to use the lesson and unit vocabulary and grammar, as well as assessing reading, writing, listening, speaking, and cultural knowledge. The on-level tests are designed to assess the language skills of most of your students. Modified tests provide more support, explanation and scaffolding to enable students with learning difficulties to produce language at the same level as their peers. Pre-AP* tests build the test-taking skills essential to success on Advanced Placement tests. The assessments for heritage learners are all in Spanish, and take into account the strengths that native speakers bring to language learning.

In addition to leveled lesson and unit tests, there is a complete array of vocabulary, culture, and grammar quizzes. All tests include scoring rubrics and point teachers to specific resources for remediation.

UNIT TRANSPARENCY BOOKS—1 PER UNIT

Each transparency book includes:

- Map Atlas Transparencies (Unit 1 only)
- Unit Opener Map Transparencies
- Fine Art Transparencies
- Vocabulary Transparencies
- Grammar Presentation Transparencies
- Situational Transparencies with Label Overlay (plus student copymasters)
- Warm Up Transparencies
- Student Book and Workbook Answer Transparencies

LECTURAS PARA TODOS

A workbook-style reader, *Lecturas para todos*, offers all the readings from the student text as well as additional literary readings in an interactive format. In addition to the readings, they contain reading strategies, comprehension questions, and tools for developing vocabulary.

There are four sections in each *Lecturas para todos*:

- *¡Avancemos!* readings with annotated skill-building support
- *Literatura adicional*—additional literary readings
- Academic and Informational Reading Development
- Test Preparation Strategies

LECTURAS PARA HISPANOHABLANTES

Lecturas para hispanohablantes offers additional cultural readings for heritage learners and a rich selection of literary readings. All readings are supported by reading strategies, comprehension questions, tools for developing vocabulary, plus tools for literary analysis.

There are four sections in each *Lecturas para hispanohablantes*:

- *En voces* cultural readings with annotated skill-building support

- *Literatura adicional*—high-interest readings by prominent authors from around the Spanish-speaking world. Selections were chosen carefully to reflect the diversity of experiences Spanish-speakers bring to the classroom.

- Bilingual Academic and Informational Reading Development

- Bilingual Test Preparation Strategies, for success on standardized tests in English

COMIC BOOKS

These fun, motivating comic books are written in a contemporary, youthful style with full-color illustrations. Each comic uses the target language students are learning. There is one 32-page comic book for each level of the program.

TPRS: TEACHING PROFICIENCY THROUGH READING AND STORYTELLING

This book includes an up-to-date guide to TPRS and TPRS stories written by Piedad Gutiérrez that use *¡Avancemos!* lesson-specific vocabulary.

MIDDLE SCHOOL RESOURCE BOOK

- Practice activities to support the 1b Bridge lesson

- Diagnostic and Bridge Unit Tests

- Transparencies
  - Vocabulary Transparencies
  - Grammar Transparencies
  - Answer Transparencies for the Student Text
  - Bridge Warm Up Transparencies

- Audio CDs

LESSON PLANS

- Lesson Plans with suggestions for modifying instruction
- Core and Expansion options clearly noted
- IEP suggested modifications
- Substitute teacher lesson plans

BEST PRACTICES TOOLKIT

Strategies for Effective Teaching

- Research-based Learning Strategies
- Language Learning that Lasts: Teaching for Long-term Retention
- Culture as a Cornerstone/Cultural Comparisons
- English Grammar Connection
- Building Vocabulary
- Developing Reading Skills
- Differentiation
- Best Practices in Teaching Heritage Learners
- Assessment (including Portfolio Assessment, Reteaching and Remediation)
- Best Practices Swap Shop: Favorite Activities for Teaching Reading, Writing, Listening, Speaking
- Reading, Writing, Listening, and Speaking Strategies in the World Languages classroom
- ACTFL Professional Development Articles
- Thematic Teaching
- Best Practices in Middle School

Using Technology in the World Languages Classroom
Tools for Motivation

- Games in the World Languages Classroom
- Teaching Proficiency through Reading and Storytelling
- Using Comic Books for Motivation

Pre-AP and International Baccalaureate

- International Baccalaureate
- Pre-AP

Graphic Organizer Transparencies

- Teaching for Long-term Retention
- Teaching Culture
- Building Vocabulary
- Developing Reading Skills

Absent Student Copymasters—Tips for Students

LISTENING TO CDS AT HOME

- Open your text, workbook, or class notes to the corresponding pages that relate to the audio you will listen to. Read the assignment directions if there are any. Do these steps before listening to the audio selections.

- Listen to the CD in a quiet place. Play the CD loudly enough so that you can hear everything clearly. Keep focused. Play a section several times until you understand it. Listen carefully. Repeat aloud with the CD. Try to sound like the people on the CD. Stop the CD when you need to do so.

- If you are lost, stop the CD. Replay it and look at your notes. Take a break if you are not focusing. Return and continue after a break. Work in short periods of time: 5 or 10 minutes at a time so that you remain focused and energized.

QUESTION/ANSWER SELECTIONS

- If there is a question/answer selection, read the question aloud several times. Write down the question. Highlight the key words, verb endings, and any new words. Look up new words and write their meaning. Then say everything aloud.

- One useful strategy for figuring out questions is to put parentheses around groups of words that go together. For example: (¿Cuántos niños)(van)(al estadio)(a las tres?) Read each group of words one at a time. Check for meaning. Write out answers. Highlight key words and verb endings. Say the question aloud. Read the answer aloud. Ask yourself if you wrote what you meant.

- Be sure to say everything aloud several times before moving on to the next question. Check for spelling, verb endings, and accent marks.

FLASHCARDS FOR VOCABULARY

- If you have Internet access, go to ClassZone at classzone.com. All the vocabulary taught in ¡Avancemos! is available on electronic flashcards. Look for the flashcards in the ¡Avancemos! section of ClassZone.

- If you don't have Internet access, write the Spanish word or phrase on one side of a 3″×5″ card, and the English translation on the other side. Illustrate your flashcards when possible. Be sure to highlight any verb endings, accent marks, or other special spellings that will need a bit of extra attention.

GRAMMAR ACTIVITIES

- Underline or highlight all verb endings and adjective agreements. For example: **Nosotros com<u>emos</u> pollo ric<u>o</u>.**

- Underline or highlight infinitive endings: **trabaj<u>ar</u>**.

- Underline or highlight accented letters. Say aloud and be louder on the accented letters. Listen carefully for the loudness. This will remind you where to write your accent mark. For example: **l<u>á</u>piz, l<u>á</u>pices, <u>á</u>rbol, <u>á</u>rboles**

- When writing a sentence, be sure to ask yourself, "What do I mean? What am I trying to say?" Then check your sentence to be sure that you wrote what you wanted to say.

- Mark patterns with a highlighter. For example, for stem-changing verbs, you can draw a "boot" around the letters that change:

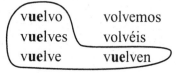

READING AND CULTURE SECTIONS

- Read the strategy box. Copy the graphic organizer so you can fill it out as you read.

- Look at the title and subtitles before you begin to read. Then look at and study any photos and read the captions. Translate the captions only if you can't understand them at all. Before you begin to read, guess what the selection will be about. What do you think that you will learn? What do you already know about this topic?

- Read any comprehension questions before beginning to read the paragraphs. This will help you focus on the upcoming reading selection. Copy the questions and highlight key words.

- Reread one or two of the questions and then go to the text. Begin to read the selection carefully. Read it again. On a sticky note, write down the appropriate question number next to where the answer lies in the text. This will help you keep track of what the questions have asked you and will help you focus when you go back to reread it later, perhaps in preparation for a quiz or test.

- Highlight any new words. Make a list or flashcards of new words. Look up their meanings. Study them. Quiz yourself or have a partner quiz you. Then go back to the comprehension questions and check your answers from memory. Look back at the text if you need to verify your answers.

PAIRED PRACTICE EXERCISES

- If there is an exercise for partners, practice both parts at home.

- If no partner is available, write out both scripts and practice both roles aloud. Highlight and underline key words, verb endings, and accent marks.

WRITING PROJECTS

- Brainstorm ideas before writing.

- Make lists of your ideas.

- Put numbers next to the ideas to determine the order in which you want to write about them.

- Group your ideas into paragraphs.

- Skip lines in your rough draft.

- Have a partner read your work and give you feedback on the meaning and language structure.

- Set it aside and reread it at least once before doing a final draft. Double-check verb endings, adjective agreements, and accents.

- Read it once again to check that you said what you meant to say.

- Be sure to have a title and any necessary illustrations or bibliography.

Did You Get It? *Presentación de vocabulario*

¡AVANZA!	**Goal:** Talk about foods and beverages.

Food and Drinks

- Food *(comidas)* and drinks *(bebidas)* can be grouped in different ways. Study the following.

Fruits	**las manzanas** *(apples)*
	las bananas *(bananas)*
	las uvas *(grapes)*
Grains	**el cereal** *(cereal)*
	el pan *(bread)*
Dairy	**el yogur** *(yogurt)*
	los huevos *(eggs)*
Meats	**la hamburguesa** *(hamburger)*
	el sándwich de jamón y queso *(ham and cheese sandwich)*
Liquids	**el café** *(coffee)*
	la sopa *(soup)*
	la leche *(milk)*
	el jugo de naranja *(orange juice)*

- Read the following dialogue to learn some ways to talk about food.

—Cuando **tengo hambre** *(I'm hungry)*, como cereal.

—Cuando **tengo sed** *(I'm thirsty)*, bebo jugo.

—Son las ocho de la mañana. ¿Por qué no comes **ahora** *(now)*?

—Sí, **tengo ganas de** *(I feel like)* comer.

—**Es importante** *(It's important)* comer **un desayuno nutritivo** *(a nutritious breakfast)*.

—Me gusta comer cereal. ¡Es muy **rico** *(delicious)*! En la cafetería **venden** *(they sell)* cereal.

—¿Y los huevos?

—No me gusta comer huevos. ¡Son **horribles** *(horrible)*! Para el desayuno, como cereal. Para el **almuerzo** *(lunch)*, como cereal. Para la **cena** *(dinner)*, ¡también como cereal!

—¿Qué? *(What?)* Es importante comer **otras** *(other)* comidas.

Did You Get It? *Práctica de vocabulario*

¡AVANZA!   **Goal:** Talk about foods and beverages.

1 Write the name of each item.

la hamburguesa	la sopa	el cereal	el pan
los huevos	la manzana	la banana	la leche

1.   2.   3.   4.

5.   6.   7.   8.

1. _____   5. _____

2. _____   6. _____

3. _____   7. _____

4. _____   8. _____

2 Which word does not belong in each group?

1. la manzana   la uva   el yogur   la banana

2. el jugo de naranja   el café   la leche   el pan

3. el desayuno   la uva   el almuerzo   la cena

4. el cereal   los huevos   el jugo de naranja   la hamburguesa

5. rico   nutritivo   horrible   la sopa

Nombre _____ Clase _____ Fecha _____

3 Choose a word from the box to complete each sentence.

hambre	sed	ganas	ricas	horrible

1. Cuando tengo _____ , como una banana.
2. Cuando tengo _____ , me gusta beber leche.
3. Tengo _____ de comer una hamburguesa.
4. Me gustan las uvas. Son muy _____ .
5. No me gusta el yogur. Es _____ .

4 Group the following into breakfast, lunch, and dinner foods and drinks. Some words can appear in more than one category.

la sopa	el yogur	el cereal	la hamburguesa	los huevos
el café	el pan	la leche	las uvas	las bananas
el jugo de naranja		las manzanas	el sándwich de jamón y queso	

El desayuno	El almuerzo	La cena

5 Complete the sentences describing what you like to eat and drink for breakfast and lunch.

1. Para el desayuno, me gusta comer _____

   y beber _____ .

2. Para el almuerzo, me gusta comer _____

   y beber _____ .

Nombre _____ Clase _____ Fecha _____

Did You Get It? *Presentación de gramática*

 Goal: Talk about things you and other people like.

Gusta vs. Gustan

- When someone likes to do something, **gustar** + infinitive is used. For example, **me gusta correr.** *(I like to run.)* Read the following sentences. They illustrate another way to use the verb **gustar**.

	Singular subject	Plural subject
(A mí)	Me **gusta** el yogur. *(I like yogurt.)*	Me **gustan** los huevos. *(I like eggs.)*
(A ti)	Te **gusta** el yogur. *(You like yogurt.)*	Te **gustan** los huevos. *(You like eggs.)*
(A usted / él / ella)	Le **gusta** el yogur. *(You / he / she likes yogurt.)*	Le **gustan** los huevos. *(You / he / she likes eggs.)*
(A nosotros/as)	Nos **gusta** el yogur. *(We like yogurt.)*	Nos **gustan** los huevos. *(We like eggs.)*
(A vosotros/as)	Os **gusta** el yogur. *(You like yogurt.)*	Os **gustan** los huevos. *(You like eggs.)*
(A ustedes / ellos / ellas)	Les **gusta** el yogur. *(You / they like yogurt.)*	Les **gustan** los huevos. *(You / they like eggs.)*

EXPLANATION: The verb **gustar** means *to like*. However, its literal meaning is *to please* or *to be pleasing to*. In the above sentences, the subjects are **el yogur** and **los huevos**. *(Yogurt pleases me / Yogurt is pleasing to me* and *Eggs please me / Eggs are pleasing to me.)* The **me, te, le, nos, os,** and **les** describe to whom something is pleasing. In other words, the singular and plural forms of **gustar** match what is liked, not the person who likes it.

- Read the dialogue to see how **gustar** is used in conversation.

  —Alicia, ¿te **gusta** la leche? *(Alice, do you like milk?)*

  —Sí, me **gusta** mucho. *(Yes, I like it a lot.)*

  —¿Y los jugos? ¿Te **gustan** los jugos? *(And juices? Do you like juices?)*

  —También me **gustan**. El jugo de naranja es muy nutritivo. *(I like them, too. Orange juice is very nutritious.)*

  —¿A tus amigos les **gusta** la leche? *(Do your friends like milk?)*

  —No, no les **gusta** la leche pero les **gustan** los jugos. *(No, they don't like milk, but they like juices.)*

  —A mí y a mis amigos nos **gustan** la leche y los jugos. ¡A nosotros nos **gusta** todo! *(My friends and I like milk and juices. We like everything!)*

Did You Get It? *Práctica de gramática*

 ¡AVANZA! **Goal:** Talk about things you and other people like.

❶ What do you like? Answer the following questions using the verb **gustar**.

   Modelo: ¿Te gusta el café? *Sí, me gusta el café.* or *No, no me gusta el café.*

   1. ¿Te gusta el pan? _____

   2. ¿Te gusta la sopa? _____

   3. ¿Te gusta el desayuno? _____

   4. ¿Te gusta la fruta? _____

   5. ¿Te gusta el sándwich de jamón y queso?

   _____

❷ What else do you like? Answer the following questions using the verb **gustar**.

   Modelo: ¿Te gustan las uvas? *Sí, me gustan las uvas.* or *No, no me gustan las uvas.*

   1. ¿Te gustan las hamburguesas? _____

   2. ¿Te gustan los huevos? _____

   3. ¿Te gustan las bananas? _____

   4. ¿Te gustan las manzanas? _____

   5. ¿Te gustan los cereales? _____

❸ Complete each sentence with **gusta** or **gustan**.

   1. Me _____ la comida.

   2. Les _____ los huevos.

   3. Te _____ el café.

   4. Nos _____ el desayuno.

   5. Les _____ las uvas.

   6. Le _____ el café.

   7. Me _____ las manzanas.

   8. Te _____ el pan.

   9. Nos _____ las hamburguesas.

   10. Les _____ la sopa.

4 Translate these sentences into English.

1. Me gusta el desayuno. _____

2. A ellos les gustan las uvas. _____

3. ¿Te gusta el café? _____

4. A ustedes les gusta el sándwich. _____

5. Nos gustan las frutas. _____

6. Te gusta la sopa. _____

7. Les gustan las manzanas. _____

8. A ella le gusta el jamón. _____

9. Me gustan los huevos. _____

10. A los chicos les gusta el yogur. _____

5 Translate these sentences into Spanish.

1. They like orange juice. _____

2. She likes cereal. _____

3. You (*pl.*) like milk. _____

4. We like yogurt. _____

5. I like grapes. _____

6. You (*sing.*) like bread. _____

7. He likes cheese. _____

8. They like eggs. _____

9. Does he like sandwiches? _____

10. We like coffee. _____

6 Use the verb **gustar** to tell what foods your family, friends, and you like.

1. A mis padres... _____

2. A mis hermanos... _____

3. A mi amigo(a)... _____

4. A todos mis amigos... _____

5. A mí... _____

Nombre _____ Clase _____ Fecha _____

Did You Get It? *Presentación de gramática*

Level 1 p. 150
Level 1A p. 168

UNIDAD 3 Lección 1   Reteaching and Practice

> **Goal:**   Learn to conjugate –er and –ir verbs.

Conjugating Regular *-er* and *-ir* Verbs

- Read the conjugations of the **-er** and **-ir** verbs.

	vender *(to sell)*	vivir *(to live)*
yo	**vendo** *(I sell)*	**vivo** *(I live)*
tú	**vendes** *(you sell)*	**vives** *(you live)*
él / ella / usted	**vende** *(he or she / you sell(s))*	**vive** *(he or she / you live(s))*
nosotros(as)	**vendemos** *(we sell)*	**vivimos** *(we live)*
vosotros(as)	**vendéis** *(you sell)*	**vivís** *(you live)*
ellos(as) / ustedes	**venden** *(they / you sell)*	**viven** *(they / you live)*

EXPLANATION: The conjugation of **-er** and **-ir** verbs is the same except in the **nosotros** and **vosotros** forms. Study the chart below. Use it as a quick reference to review and compare the conjugation of all three verb forms.

-ar		-er		-ir	
-o	-amos	-o	-emos	-o	-imos
-as	-áis	-es	-éis	-es	-ís
-a	-an	-e	-en	-e	-en

Did You Get It? *Práctica de gramática*

> ¡AVANZA! **Goal:** Learn to conjugate –er and –ir verbs.

❶ Write the correct form of **correr** based on the subject.

1. tú _____

2. ellos _____

3. usted _____

4. yo _____

5. Paco _____

6. ustedes _____

7. Ana _____

8. Andrés y yo _____

❷ Write the correct form of **escribir** based on the subject.

1. los estudiantes _____

2. nosotros _____

3. ella _____

4. ustedes _____

5. tú _____

6. yo _____

7. usted _____

8. él _____

❸ Complete each sentence with the correct form of the verb in parentheses.

1. Delia _____ en los Estados Unidos. (**vivir**)

2. Karen y yo _____ paella. (**comer**)

3. Ana _____ todos los días. (**correr**)

4. Ellas _____ mucha leche. (**beber**)

5. Tú _____ un libro. (**leer**)

6. Emiliana _____ el desayuno. (**compartir**)

7. Rodrigo _____ inglés. (**aprender**)

8. Nosotros _____ frutas. (**comer**)

9. Ellos _____ comida en la cafetería. (**vender**)

10. Yo _____ en los Estados Unidos. (**vivir**)

Nombre _____ Clase _____ Fecha _____

4 Form sentences using the words and expressions given. Follow the model.

Modelo: Andrés / beber jugo / para el desayuno
Andrés bebe jugo para el desayuno.

1. Lucía y yo / aprender español / en la escuela

   _____

2. los chicos / correr / todos los días

   _____

3. ustedes / compartir una pizza / en la cafetería

   _____

4. tú / leer un libro / en la biblioteca

   _____

5. yo / escribir en el pizarrón / en clase

   _____

6. nosotros / comer un sándwich / para el almuerzo

   _____

7. ellos / vender fruta / en la cafetería

   _____

8. Alicia y Jorge / escribir correos electrónicos / en la computadora

   _____

5 Complete the sentences. Use each verb in the box at least once.

beber	comer	compartir	escribir	leer	vender	vivir

1. Mi amigo _____
2. Mi amiga _____
3. Los directores _____
4. Todos mis amigos _____
5. Mi maestro(a) de español _____
6. Yo _____

 **¿Recuerdas?**

Gustar + infinitive

- Read the following examples of using **gustar** + infinitive.

> **¿Te gusta hablar** español? *(Do you like to speak Spanish?)*
> Sí, a mí **me gusta hablar** español. *(Yes, I like to speak Spanish.)*

> ¿A la maestra **le gusta enseñar**? *(Does the teacher like to teach?)*
> Sí, a ella **le gusta enseñar**. *(Yes, she likes to teach.)*

Práctica

Write sentences telling what each person likes to do.

Modelo: ellas / comprar

A ellas les gusta comprar.

1. él / correr

_____

2. usted / aprender español

_____

3. yo / descansar

_____

4. Miguel y yo / alquilar películas

_____

5. las chicas / escribir correos electrónicos

_____

6. mis amigos / andar en patineta

_____

7. Amalia / pasar un rato con los amigos

_____

8. tú / leer un libro

_____

9. ustedes / compartir el almuerzo

_____

10. nosotros / hablar español

_____

Nombre _____ Clase _____ Fecha _____

♻ ¿Recuerdas?

Snack Foods

• Study the following words for snack foods.

Las comidas *(Foods)*	**la fruta**	*(fruit)*
	las papas fritas	*(French fries)*
	la galleta	*(cookie)*
	el helado	*(ice cream)*
	la pizza	*(pizza)*
Las bebidas *(Drinks)*	**el agua**	*(water)*
	el jugo	*(juice)*
	el refresco	*(soft drink)*

Práctica

❶ Write the name of these foods or drinks.

1.　　　2.　　　3.　　　4.　　　5.　　　6.

1. _____　　4. _____

2. _____　　5. _____

3. _____　　6. _____

❷ Name three of your favorite snacks.

1. _____

2. _____

3. _____

UNIDAD 3 Lección 1

Reteaching and Practice

 ¿Recuerdas?

The Verb *estar* (*to be*)

The verb **estar** is used to say *where* a person or thing is.

Yo **estoy** en la clase.	*I am in the classroom.*
Tú **estás** en la cafetería.	*You are in the cafeteria.*
Él (Ella, Usted) **está** en el gimnasio.	*He (She, You) is (are) in the gym.*
Nosotros **estamos** en la oficina.	*We are in the office.*
Ellos (Ellas, Ustedes) **están** en el pasillo.	*They (You) are in the hall.*
Vosotros (Vosotras) **estáis** en la biblioteca.	*You are in the library.*

EXPLANATION: The verb **estar** is another way to say *to be*. Use it to say *where* somebody is.

Práctica

1 Complete the sentences using the correct form of **estar**.

1. Tú _____ en la clase.
2. Tus amigos _____ en la clase.
3. Usted _____ en la clase.
4. Ana y Rosita _____ en la clase.
5. Juan _____ en la clase.
6. Yo _____ en la clase.
7. Luis y yo _____ en la clase.
8. Ustedes _____ en la clase.

Telling time

To say what time it is, use **es** or **son**.

Es la una.	*It is one o'clock.*
Son las dos.	*It is two o'clock.*
Son las cuatro **y** diez.	*It is ten minutes past four.*
Son las ocho **menos** cinco.	*It is five minutes to eight.*
Son las nueve **menos cuarto**.	*It is quarter to nine.*
Son las once **y media**.	*It is eleven-thirty.*

EXPLANATION: To say it is one o'clock, use **es**. To say any other time, use **son**. To say it is some time *after* the hour, use **y**. To say it is some time *before* the hour, use **menos**. **Cuarto** means a *quarter* of an hour and **media** means *half* an hour.

Práctica

1 Tell what time it is in each case.

1. _____ (3:00)
2. _____ (12:30)
3. _____ (1:30)
4. _____ (3:45)
5. _____ (4:15)
6. _____ (8:50)

Did You Get It? *Presentación de vocabulario*

> ¡AVANZA!   **Goal:**   Talk about family.

The Family

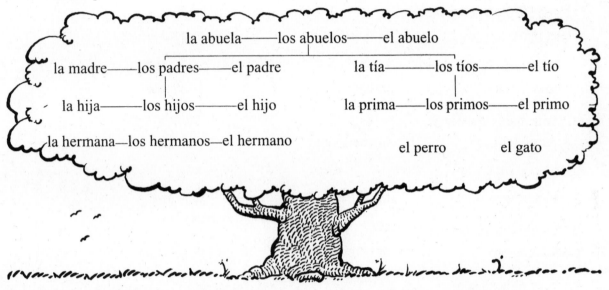

la abuela——los abuelos——el abuelo

la madre——los padres——el padre   la tía——los tíos——el tío

la hija——los hijos——el hijo   la prima——los primos——el primo

la hermana—los hermanos—el hermano

el perro   el gato

- Study the names of the months (**los meses**) in Spanish. Then read the dialogue at the bottom to learn how to ask about the date.

enero	*(January)*	**mayo**	*(May)*	**septiembre**	*(September)*
febrero	*(February)*	**junio**	*(June)*	**octubre**	*(October)*
marzo	*(March)*	**julio**	*(July)*	**noviembre**	*(November)*
abril	*(April)*	**agosto**	*(August)*	**diciembre**	*(December)*

—¿**Cuál es la fecha de hoy?** *(What's today's date?)*
—**Es el primero de enero.** *(It's the first of January.)*

- Here are some more numbers (**números**).

doscientos	*(200)*	**setecientos**	*(700)*
trescientos	*(300)*	**ochocientos**	*(800)*
cuatrocientos	*(400)*	**novecientos**	*(900)*
quinientos	*(500)*	**mil**	*(1000)*
seiscientos	*(600)*	**un millón (de)**	*(1,000,000 (of))*

- Here are some ways to talk about how old someone is.

—**Yo tengo quince años.** *(I am 15 years old.)*
—¿**Cuántos años tienes tú?** *(How old are you?)*

Did You Get It? *Práctica de vocabulario*

¡AVANZA! **Goal:** Talk about family.

1 Who is . . .

1. the family's pet feline?

el perro   la familia   el gato

2. your father's daughter?

tu prima   tu hermana   tu abuela

3. your father's sisters?

tus abuelos   tus hermanas   tus tías

4. your uncle's son?

tu hermano   tu padre   tu primo

5. your mother's father?

tu abuelo   tu padre   tu hermano

6. your father's son?

tu prima   tu hermano   tu abuela

7. your mother's children?

tus hermanos   tus tías   tus hijos

8. the family's pet canine?

el gato   el perro   la familia

9. your grandmother's son?

tu hijo   tu padre   tu hermano

10. your aunt's daughter?

tu abuela   tu tía   tu prima

2 In which month . . .

1. is Valentine's day? _____

2. does the New Year begin? _____

3. is Halloween? _____

4. is Independence Day? _____

5. does summer begin? _____

3 Answer the questions in Spanish. Follow the model.

    Modelo: ¿Quiénes son las hermanas de tu padre?

               Son mis tías.

    1. ¿Quién es el padre de tu madre? _____

    2. ¿Quién es la hija de tu padre? _____

    3. ¿Quién es la hija de tu tío? _____

    4. ¿Quién es la madre de tu padre? _____

    5. ¿Quiénes son los hijos de tu tía? _____

4 Answer these questions in Spanish.

    1. ¿Cuál es la fecha de hoy? _____

    2. ¿Cuántos hermanos tienes? _____

    3. ¿Cuántos años tienen tus hermanos? _____

    4. ¿Cuándo es el cumpleaños de tu hermano(a)? _____

    5. ¿Cuántos años tienes tú? _____

    6. ¿Cuándo es tu cumpleaños? _____

5 Draw your family tree or a family tree of a famous family and label it in Spanish.

Did You Get It? *Presentación de gramática*

¡AVANZA!	**Goal:** Learn about possessive adjectives.

Possessive Adjectives

- **Number Agreement.** Possessive adjectives describe a relationship between people or things. Read the following sentences, paying attention to the boldfaced words.

Mi abuela tiene 60 años.	(**My** grandmother is 60 years old.)
Mis abuelos tienen 60 años.	(**My** grandparents are 60 years old.)
Tu padre tiene 40 años.	(**Your** father is 40 years old.)
Tus padres tienen 40 años.	(**Your** parents are 40 years old.)
Su tío tiene 35 años.	(**His** or **her / your / their** uncle is 35 years old.)
Sus tíos tienen 35 años.	(**His** or **her / your / their** uncles are 35 years old.)

EXPLANATION: In Spanish, possessive adjectives agree in number with the nouns they describe. They agree with what is possessed, not with the person who possesses it.

- **Gender Agreement.** Read the sentences, paying attention to the boldfaced words.

Nuestra madre es maestra.	(**Our** mother is a teacher.)
Nuestros padres son maestras.	(**Our** parents are teachers.)
Nuestro padre es maestro.	(**Our** father is a teacher.)
Nuestras tías son maestras.	(**Our** aunts are teachers.)

EXPLANATION: The adjectives **nuestro** and **vuestro** have both masculine and feminine forms. They agree in gender with the nouns they describe. Remember that they also agree in number. Study the following table and use it as a quick reference for possessive adjectives.

Singular Possessive Adjectives		Plural Possessive Adjectives	
mi *my*	**nuestro(a)** *our*	mis *my*	**nuestros(as)** *our*
tu *your (familiar)*	**vuestro(a)** *your (familiar)*	tus *your (familiar)*	**vuestros(as)** *your (familiar)*
su *your (formal)*	su *your (formal)*	sus *your (formal)*	sus *your (formal)*
su *his, her, its*	su *their*	sus *his, her, its*	sus *their*

Nombre _____ Clase _____ Fecha _____

Did You Get It? *Práctica de gramática*

Level 1 pp. 170–171
Level 1A pp. 191–193

 Goal: Learn about possessive adjectives.

1 Match each English phrase with its corresponding Spanish phrase.

1. sus zapatos　　　　your grandfather
2. su abuelo　　　　　my cousin
3. mi escuela　　　　　his shoes
4. mi primo　　　　　　our grandmother
5. nuestra abuela　　　my school
6. mis zapatos　　　　　your grandparents
7. tus abuelos　　　　　my shoes

2 Fill in the correct possessive adjectives.

1. _____ libro *(his)*
2. _____ padre *(our)*
3. _____ abuelos *(their)*
4. _____ primas *(your, familiar sing.)*
5. _____ familia *(your, familiar sing.)*
6. _____ primos *(our)*
7. _____ gatos *(my)*

3 Write the appropriate possessive adjective for each sentence.

1. _____ primo se llama Miguel. *(our)*
2. _____ hermano es inteligente. *(her)*
3. _____ tía es creativa. *(my)*
4. _____ abuelo es serio. *(her)*
5. _____ abuelos son mayores. *(your, familiar sing., in L.A.)*
6. _____ calculadora está debajo del escritorio. *(his)*
7. _____ lápiz es amarillo. *(his)*
8. _____ mochilas son grandes. *(their)*

UNIDAD 3 Lección 2　Reteaching and Practice

¡Avancemos! 1
Unit Resource Book

Unidad 3, Lección 2
Reteaching and Practice **17**

4 Translate the following sentences into Spanish.

1. José is my brother.

_____

2. María is your sister. *(your, formal)*

_____

3. Your dog's name is Lacy. *(your, familiar sing.)*

_____

4. Our grandfather's birthday is January 4th.

_____

5. Your uncle likes apples. *(your, familiar sing.)*

_____

6. His grandfather's name is José.

_____

7. Our house is large.

_____

8. Their parents work a lot.

_____

9. My cat is pretty.

_____

10. My aunt is a teacher.

_____

5 Write a short paragraph describing your family or a friend's family. Use as many possessive adjectives as you can.

Modelo: *Tengo dos hermanos. Mi hermano, Pablo, tiene diez años. Su cumpleaños*
es el primero de enero. Mi hermana, Alicia, tiene ocho años. Su cumpleaños
es el cuatro de abril.

_____

_____

_____

_____

_____

_____

_____

Did You Get It? *Presentación de gramática*

> ¡AVANZA! **Goal:** Learn to compare things and people.

Making Comparisons

- There are several phrases in Spanish used to make comparisons. Read the following sentences, paying attention to the boldfaced words and underlined letters.

Álvaro es **más simpático que** Luis.	*(Álvaro is **more pleasant than** Luis.)*
Mónica es **menos divertida que** Carolina.	*(Mónica is **less fun than** Carolina.)*
Los chicos son **tan serios como** la maestra.	*(The boys are **as serious as** the teacher.)*

EXPLANATION: Sometimes, we use an adjective to compare two things. The adjective agrees with the noun that comes before it.

- Now read these sentences, paying attention to the boldfaced words.

Me gusta ir a la cafetería **más que** al gimnasio.	*(I like to go to the cafeteria **more than** to the gym.)*
Me gustan las bananas **menos que** las fresas.	*(I like bananas **less than** strawberries.)*
Me gusta caminar **tanto como** correr.	*(I like to walk **as much as** run.)*

EXPLANATION: Comparisons do not always include an adjective.

- Now read these sentences, paying attention to the boldfaced words.

Mi tía es **mayor que** mi tío.	*(My aunt is **older than** my uncle.)*
Mi madre es **menor que** mi padre.	*(My mother is **younger than** my father.)*
Mis abuelos son **mayores que** mis padres.	*(My grandparents are **older than** my parents.)*

EXPLANATION: There are a few irregular comparative words. Study the chart below and use it as a quick reference.

	Singular	Plural
older —→	**mayor**	**mayores**
younger —→	**menor**	**menores**
better —→	**mejor**	**mejores**
worse —→	**peor**	**peores**

Did You Get It? *Práctica de gramática*

> **¡AVANZA!**　**Goal:**　Learn to compare things and people.

❶ Complete the following sentences with **que** or **como**.

1. Julián es más organizado _____ su vecino.

2. Matilde es tan inteligente _____ su hermana.

3. Elena corre tanto _____ José.

4. Pedro tiene más libros _____ su amigo.

5. Sara toca la guitarra mejor _____ su hermano.

6. Ricardo es tan trabajador _____ su hermano.

❷ Form sentences by matching the following.

1. Jorge es tan guapo...　　　　　　　que su tía.

2. Alisa es más bonita...　　　　　　　que las hamburguesas.

3. A ellos les gusta hablar tanto...　　como su hermano.

4. A mí me gusta la sopa menos...　　que estudiar.

5. Leer es más divertido...　　　　　　como escuchar.

❸ Choose the sentence that describes each picture.

1.	2.	3.	4.	5.

mi tía **mi abuela**	**los chicos**　**las chicas**	**Mónica**　**Alicia**	**Marco**　**Arturo**	**Marta**

1. **a.** Mi tía es mayor que mi abuela.
   b. Mi tía es menor que mi abuela.

2. **a.** Las chicas son menos serias que los chicos.
   b. Las chicas son más serias que los chicos.

3. **a.** Mónica es más estudiosa que Alicia.
   b. Alicia es tan estudiosa como Mónica.

4. **a.** Marco es más alto que Arturo.
   b. Arturo es tan alto como Marco.

5. **a.** A Marta le gusta descansar más que correr.
   b. A Marta le gusta descansar menos que correr.

4 Write four sentences using some of the comparative expressions from the box. Follow the model.

más... que	tan... como	mayor(es)	mejor(es)
menos... que	tanto... como	menor(es)	peor(es)

Modelo: bananas / manzanas

Me gustan las bananas más que las manzanas.

1. hermano / padre

_____

2. la clase de español / la clase de inglés

_____

3. tú / tu amigo(a)

_____

4. tus primos / tú

_____

5 Translate the following sentences into Spanish using the correct form of the comparative expression in parentheses.

1. Marcia is taller than Tomás. _(más... que)_

_____

2. Delia is less studious than her sister. _(menos... que)_

_____

3. The boys are as intelligent as the girls. _(tan... como)_

_____

4. I like to go to the cafeteria more than to the gym. _(más que)_

_____

5. My parents are older than my aunts and uncles. _(mayor que)_

_____

6. The bananas are better than the grapes. _(mejor que)_

_____

7. The soup is worse than the yogurt. _(peor que)_

_____

¿Recuerdas?

The verb tener

- Review the conjugation of the verb **tener** *(to have)*.

Tener *(to have)*	
Singular	**Plural**
yo **tengo** *(I have)*	nosotros(as) **tenemos** *(we have)*
tú **tienes** *(you have)*	vosotros(as) **tenéis** *(you have)*
usted **tiene** *(you have)*	ustedes **tienen** *(you have)*
él **tiene** *(he has)*	ellos **tienen** *(they have)*
ella **tiene** *(she has)*	ellas **tienen** *(they have)*

Práctica

Form sentences about age using the words and ages given. Follow the model.

Modelo: la abuela / 58

_____ *La abuela tiene cincuenta y ocho años.* _____

1. el abuelo / 70

_____

2. sus padres / 45

_____

3. su hermano menor / 9

_____

4. Alejandro y yo / 18

_____

5. yo / 16

_____

✿ ¿Recuerdas?

Numbers from 11 to 100

- Study the numbers from 11 to 100.

once	11	veinte	20	treinta	30
doce	12	veintiuno	21	treinta y uno	31
trece	13	veintidós	22	cuarenta	40
catorce	14	veintitrés	23	cincuenta	50
quince	15	veinticuatro	24	sesenta	60
dieciséis	16	veinticinco	25	setenta	70
diecisiete	17	veintiséis	26	ochenta	80
dieciocho	18	veintisiete	27	noventa	90
diecinueve	19	veintiocho	28	cien	100
		veintinueve	29		

Práctica

Solve the math problems in Spanish.

1. $22 - 10 =$ _____
2. $32 + 8 =$ _____
3. $22 \times 2 =$ _____
4. $60 \div 2 =$ _____
5. $45 - 3 =$ _____
6. $50 + 10 =$ _____
7. $64 + 36 =$ _____
8. $95 - 5 =$ _____
9. $25 + 12 =$ _____
10. $75 \times 1 =$ _____
11. $100 \div 2 =$ _____
12. $56 - 34 =$ _____
13. $22 \times 3 =$ _____
14. $32 - 14 =$ _____
15. $98 - 17 =$ _____

¿Recuerdas?

After-school activities

- Read the after-school activities listed below.

    correr *(to run)*

    escribir correos electrónicos *(to write emails)*

    escuchar música *(to listen to music)*

    hacer la tarea *(to do homework)*

    leer libros *(to read books)*

    mirar la televisión *(to watch television)*

    pasar un rato con los amigos *(to spend time with friends)*

    pasear *(to go for a walk)*

    practicar deportes *(to play sports)*

    preparar la comida *(to prepare food / a meal)*

    tocar la guitarra *(to play the guitar)*

    trabajar *(to work)*

Práctica

Which activity would the following people most likely do based on the descriptions? Some people may do more than one activity. Follow the model.

    Modelo: Elena es estudiosa.

          Ella lee libros.

1. El padre de Arturo es trabajador.

_____

2. La hermana de Andrea es perezosa.

_____

3. Los chicos son atléticos.

_____

4. Luis no es perezoso.

_____

5. Ana y Enrique son simpáticos.

_____

Did You Get It? Answer Key

PRÁCTICA DE VOCABULARIO

Food and Drinks, pp. 2–3

❶

1.	la manzana	2.	la hamburguesa
3.	el cereal	4.	el pan
5.	la sopa	6.	la leche
7.	los huevos	8.	la banana

❷

1.	el yogur	2.	el pan
3.	la uva	4.	la hamburguesa
5.	la sopa		

❸

1. hambre
2. sed
3. ganas
4. ricas
5. horrible

❹ Answers will vary. Possible answers:

la sopa: el almuerzo, la cena

la hamburguesa: el almuerzo, la cena

el café: el desayuno

los huevos: el desayuno

el yogur: el desayuno

las uvas: el desayuno, el almuerzo

el pan: el almuerzo, la cena

las bananas: el desayuno, el almuerzo

el cereal: el desayuno

las manzanas: el desayuno, el almuerzo

la leche: el desayuno el almuerzo

el sándwich de jamón y queso: el almuerzo, la cena

el jugo de naranja: el desayuno

❺ Answers will vary.

PRÁCTICA DE GRAMÁTICA

Gusta vs. Gustan, pp. 5–6

❶

1. Sí, me gusta el pan. / No, no me gusta el pan.
2. Sí, me gusta la sopa. / No, no me gusta la sopa.
3. Sí, me gusta el desayuno. / No, no me gusta el desayuno.
4. Sí, me gusta la fruta. / No, no me gusta la fruta.
5. Sí, me gusta el sándwich de jamón y queso. / No, no me gusta el sándwich de jamón y queso.

❷

1. Sí, me gustan las hamburguesas. / No, no me gustan las hamburguesas.
2. Sí, me gustan los huevos. / No, no me gustan los huevos.
3. Sí, me gustan las bananas. / No, no me gustan las bananas.
4. Sí, me gustan las manzanas. / No, no me gustan las manzanas.
5. Sí, me gustan los cereales. / No, no me gustan los cereales.

❸

1.	gusta	2.	gustan
3.	gusta	4.	gusta
5.	gustan	6.	gusta
7.	gustan	8.	gusta
9.	gustan	10.	gusta

Did You Get It? Answer Key

❹
1. I like breakfast.
2. They like grapes.
3. Do you like coffee?
4. You like the sandwich.
5. We like fruits.
6. You like soup.
7. You like apples.
8. She likes ham.
9. I like eggs.
10. The boys like yogurt.

❺
1. Les gusta el jugo de naranja.
2. Le gusta el cereal.
3. Os/Les gusta la leche.
4. Nos gusta el yogur.
5. Me gustan las uvas.
6. Te/Le gusta el pan.
7. Le gusta el queso.
8. Les gustan los huevos.
9. ¿Le gustan los sándwiches?
10. Nos gusta el café.

❻ Answers will vary.

PRÁCTICA DE GRAMÁTICA

Conjugating Regular -er and -ir Verbs, pp. 8–9

❶
1. corres	2. corren	3. corre
4. corro	5. corre	6. corren
7. corre	8. corremos	

❷
1. escriben	2. escribimos	3. escribe
4. escriben	5. escribes	6. escribo
7. escribe	8. escribe	

❸
1. vive		2. comemos
3. corre		4. beben
5. lees		6. comparte
7. aprende		8. comemos
9. venden		10. vivo

❹
1. Lucía y yo aprendemos español en la escuela.
2. Los chicos corren todos los días.
3. Ustedes comparten una pizza en la cafetería.
4. Tú lees un libro en la biblioteca.
5. Yo escribo en el pizarrón en clase.
6. Nosotros comemos un sándwich para el almuerzo.
7. Ellos venden fruta en la cafetería.
8. Alicia y Jorge escriben correos electrónicos en la computadora.

❺ Answers will vary.

✺ ¿RECUERDAS?
Gustar + infinitive, p. 10

Práctica
1. A él le gusta correr.
2. A usted le gusta aprender español.
3. A mí me gusta descansar.
4. A Miguel y a mí nos gusta alquilar películas.
5. A las chicas les gusta escribir correos electrónicos.
6. A mis amigos les gusta andar en patineta.

Did You Get It? Answer Key

7. A Amalia le gusta pasar un rato con los amigos.

8. A ti te gusta leer un libro.

9. A ustedes les gusta compartir el almuerzo.

10. A nosotros nos gusta hablar español.

 ¿RECUERDAS?

Snack Foods, p. 11

Práctica

1

1. el helado
2. la galleta
3. el jugo de naranja
4 las papas fritas
5. la pizza
6. la fruta

2 Answers will vary.

 ¿RECUERDAS?

*The Verb **estar** (to be), Telling Time, p. 12*

1

1. estás	5. está
2. están	6. estoy
3. está	7. estamos
4. están	8. están

2

1. Son las tres.
2. Son las doce y media.
3. Es la una y media.
4. Son las cuatro menos cuarto.
5. Son las cuatro y cuarto.
6. Son las nueve menos diez.

Did You Get It? Answer Key

PRÁCTICA DE VOCABULARIO

The Family, pp. 14–15

❶

1. el gato
2. tu hermana
3. tus tías
4. tu primo
5. tu abuelo
6. tu hermano
7. tus hermanos
8. el perro
9. tu padre
10. tu prima

❷

1. febrero
2. enero
3. octubre
4. julio
5. junio

❸

1. Es mi abuelo.
2. Es mi hermana.
3. Es mi prima.
4. Es mi abuela.
5. Son mis primos.

❹

1. Hoy es el...
2. Tengo...
3. Mi hermano mayor tiene...
4. El cumpleaños de mi hermano(a) es el...
5. Tengo...
6. Mi cumpleaños es el...

❺ Answers will vary.

PRÁCTICA DE GRAMÁTICA

Possessive Adjectives, pp. 17–18

❶

1. sus zapatos—his shoes
2. su abuelo—your grandfather
3. mi escuela—my school
4. mi primo—my cousin
5. nuestra abuela—our grandmother
6. mis zapatos—my shoes
7. tus abuelos—your grandparents

❷

1. su
2. nuestro
3. sus
4. tus
5. tu
6. nuestros
7. mis

❸

1. Nuestro
2. Su
3. Mi
4. Su
5. Tus
6. Su
7. Su
8. Sus

❹

1. José es mi hermano.
2. María es su hermana.
3. Tu perro se llama Lacy.
4. El cumpleaños de nuestro abuelo es el 4 de enero.
5. A tu tío le gustan las manzanas.
6. Su abuelo se llama José.
7. Nuestra casa es grande.
8. Sus padres trabajan mucho.
9. Mi gato es bonito.
10. Mi tía es maestra.

❺ Answers will vary.

Did You Get It? Answer Key

PRÁCTICA DE GRAMÁTICA
Making Comparisons, pp. 20–21

❶

1. que
2. como
3. como
4. que
5. que
6. como

❷

1. Jorge es tan guapo... como su hermano.
2. Alisa es más bonita... que su tía.
3. A ellos les gusta hablar tanto... como escuchar.
4. A mí me gusta la sopa menos... que las hamburguesas.
5. Leer es más divertido ... que estudiar.

❸

1. **b.** Mi tía es menor que mi abuela.
2. **b.** Las chicas son más serias que los chicos.
4. **a.** Mónica es más estudiosa que Alicia.
5. **a.** Marco es más alto que Arturo.
6. **a.** A Ana le gusta descansar más que correr.

❹ Answers will vary.

❺

1. Marcia es más alta que Tomás.
2. Delia es menos estudiosa que su hermana.
3. Los chicos son tan inteligentes como las chicas.
4. Me gusta ir a la cafetería más que al gimnasio.
5. Mis padres son mayores que mis tíos.
6. Las bananas son mejores que las uvas.
7. La sopa es peor que el yogur.

¿RECUERDAS?
The Verb **tener***, p. 22*

Práctica

1. El abuelo tiene setenta años.
2. Sus padres tienen cuarenta y cinco años.
3. Su hermano menor tiene nueve años.
4. Alejandro y yo tenemos dieciocho años.
5. Yo tengo dieciséis años.

¿RECUERDAS?
Numbers from 11 to 100, p. 23

Práctica

1. doce
2. cuarenta
3. cuarenta y cuatro
4. treinta
5. cuarenta y dos
6. sesenta
7. cien
8. noventa
9. treinta y siete
10. setenta y cinco
11. cincuenta
12. veintidós
13. sesenta y seis
14. dieciocho
15. ochenta y uno

Did You Get It? Answer Key

 **¿RECUERDAS?**

After-school Activities, p. 24

Práctica

1. Él trabaja mucho.
2. Ella descansa mucho. Ella mira mucho la televisión.
3. Ellos practican deportes. Ellos corren.
4. Él trabaja mucho. / Él lee libros. / Él hace la tarea. / Practica deportes.
5. Ellos pasan un rato con los amigos. / Ellos escriben correos electrónicos.

Crucigrama *Práctica de vocabulario*

Identify the food pictured and use the clues to complete the puzzle.

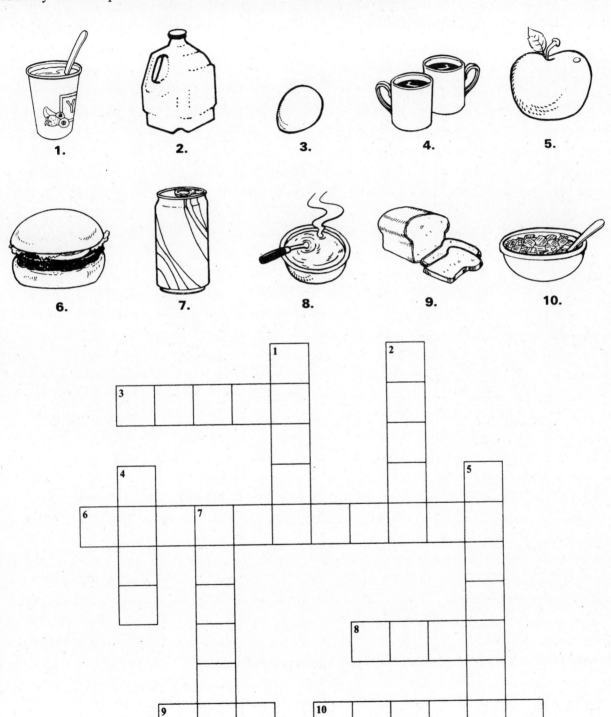

1.

2.

3.

4.

5.

6.

7.

8.

9.

10.

UNIDAD 3 Lección 1. Practice Games

El paseo *Vocabulario en contexto*

Your class went on a field trip to a farm to learn about food production. Write the name of the food items from the **Vocabulario** that come from what is shown in each picture. Some have more than one answer.

1. _____

_____

_____

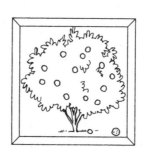

2. _____

_____

_____

3. _____

_____

_____

4. _____

_____

_____

5. _____

_____

_____

6. _____

_____

_____

Bonus: Which item above gets the award for most food produced?

UNIDAD 3 Lección 1

Practice Games

Rimas *Práctica de gramática 1*

Read the following poem and circle all of the singular nouns, then list them below.
Put a rectangle around all of the plural nouns, and then list them below. Complete the
poem by filling in the blanks to describe things that you like.

A Javier le gustan las manzanas.
Las come todas las mañanas.
A Lila le gusta el café.
Siempre lo bebe con leche.

A Pilar le gustan las naranjas.
Las come con bananas.
A David le gusta un huevo.
Le gusta el huevo con queso.

A mí me gustan _____ .
Me gustan todos los días.

A mí me gusta _____ .
¡Tengo hambre!

Plural nouns: _____

Singular nouns: _____

Nombre _____ Clase _____ Fecha _____

¿Me gusta? ¿Te gusta? ¿Le gusta? *Gramática en contexto*

Use the phrases to form correct sentences below and help the Meléndez family figure out what to have for lunch.

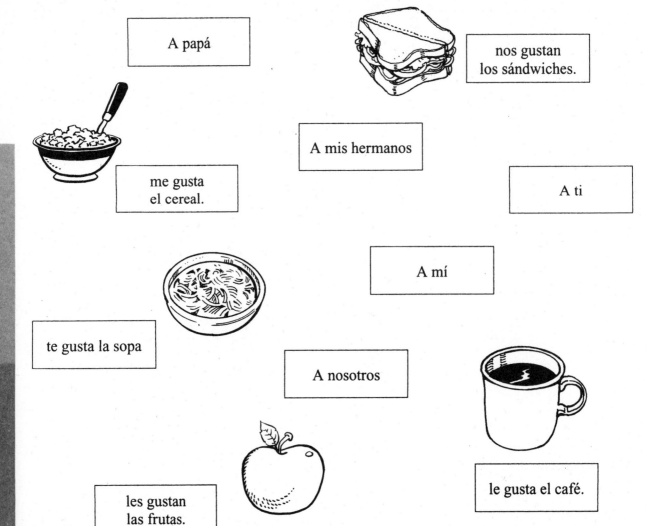

_____
_____
_____
_____
_____

Parejas *Práctica de gramática 2*

First, identify the following two-word combinations from the **Vocabulario**, using the letters given as clues. Then, use the completed words to figure out the answer to the bonus question.

1. ___ ___ ___ ayu ___ o y ___ af ___
  1   2   3   4   5   6

2. hu ___ ___ ___ y p ___ n
        7   8   9   10

3. u ___ ___ s y ___ ___ gu ___
        11   12   13   14   15

4. ___ a ___ ___ urg ___ ___ ___ a h ___ r ___ ___ ble
        16   17   18   19   20   21   22   23   24

5. ___ om ___ d ___ y ___ e ___ ___ da
        25   26   27   28   29   30

BONUS: ¡Tenemos hambre! Tenemos ganas de comer

___ ___ ___ ___ ___ ___   ___ ___ ___ ___
25   22   17   30   1   12   23   26   5   10

¿Qué vas a servir? *Todo junto*

You're having some friends over for lunch. However, you know that your friends don't all like the same foods. Figure out what you can serve, after you determine what they like and don't like.

1. A Mario le gustan las hamburguesas y las uvas. No le gustan las bananas. Mario no puede comer los helados.

2. A Susana le gustan las uvas pero no le gustan los huevos.

3. A Rodrigo le gusta la sopa, las hamburguesas y la pizza. No le gustan los helados.

4. A Marisol le gustan los helados y las hamburguesas pero no le gusta la pizza. Marisol no puede tomar leche.

5. A todos les gustan las manzanas, los refrescos y los jugos.

6. A nadie le gusta el jamón.

¿Qué puedes servirles a tus amigos?

El menú para nuestro almuerzo:

_____

_____

_____

_____

_____

UNIDAD 3 Lección 1

Practice Games

Unidad 3, Lección 1
Practice Games

36

¡Avancemos! 1
Unit Resource Book

Sopa de letras *Lectura cultural*

Find the seven breakfast foods from the **Vocabulario** hidden in the word search.
Highlight the foods you like in one color and the foods you dislike in another color.
Write the names of the foods on the lines below.

```
L  B  M  A  E  N  J  É  Y  X  Y  X  A  Y
A  B  C  Z  O  H  U  A  R  C  G  E  H  I
G  J  A  Z  W  U  J  G  M  B  R  C  N  C
A  B  F  I  R  E  O  É  J  Z  P  M  Y  Y
L  A  É  P  A  V  D  C  E  R  E  A  L  O
L  C  M  A  S  O  E  Q  N  R  Y  C  E  G
E  T  M  L  B  S  N  H  T  Y  E  O  C  U
T  Y  V  V  I  B  G  P  R  R  G  S  H  R
J  U  G  O  D  E  N  A  R  A  N  J  A  S
O  D  A  L  E  H  L  N  J  A  G  P  S  P
M  O  L  E  C  H  E  F  L  F  L  D  O  A
K  V  Z  K  V  C  É  R  C  S  X  B  S  P
```

_____   _____

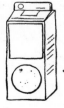

_____   _____

UNIDAD 3 Lección 1   Practice Games

El oráculo *Repaso*

You found a crystal ball that produces images to help you read minds. See what your friends feel like doing when they hold the ball. Write a complete sentence using the correct form of **tener ganas de** for each person that describes what they feel like doing.

1.   2.   3.   4.

5.   6.   7.

1. Carlos y Pablo _____

2. Ana _____

3. Marcos y yo _____

4. Isabel y tú _____

5. Paula _____

6. Yo _____

7. Tú _____

Equipos mixtos *Práctica de vocabulario*

Many people want to play soccer at Raúl's family picnic. Help Raúl divide his
family members into teams by age: even ages on one team and odd ages on the other.
Write the names and ages of the family members on each team in the roster below.

1. Raúl tiene catorce años.

2. Su primo Javier tiene tres años más que Raúl.

3. Papá tiene veinte años más que Javier.

4. Elisa tiene diez y siete años menos que Papá.

5. Tío Cristián tiene catorce años más que Elisa.

6. Mamá tiene cuatro años más que Cristián.

7. La hermana de Raúl Inés tiene diez y ocho años menos que Mamá.

8. Tía Diana tiene treinta y un años más que Inés.

9. Celia tiene seis años menos que Diana.

10. Alejandro tiene diez y seis años menos que Celia.

11. Melinda tiene trece años menos que Alejandro.

12. Juan tiene diez y seis años más que Melinda.

13. Abuelo tiene treinta y un años más que Juan.

14. Gregorio tiene treinta y seis años menos que Abuelo.

Team Odd	Team Even
1. _____	1. _____
2. _____	2. _____
3. _____	3. _____
4. _____	4. _____
5. _____	5. _____
6. _____	6. _____
7. _____	7. _____

Comparativos escondidos *Vocabulario en contexto*

Find the comparative phrase or word that is hidden in each sentence. Hint: you will
have to look in all the words to find each answer.

Modelo: Es para nosotros. ____ ____ ____ ____

      Es para n**os**otros. *peor*

1. Mira el pelirrojo. ____ ____ ____ ____ ____

2. Mi abuela quiere sopa. ____ ____ ____ ____ ____ ____

3. Como pan nutritivo. ____ ____ ____ ____ ____ ____ ____ ____ ____

4. Compramos hoy. ____ ____ ____ ____ ____

5. Contesta problemas. ____ ____ ____ ____ ____

6. Norman es pequeño. ____ ____ ____ ____ ____ ____ ____ ____

El sol, la luna, las estrellas *Práctica de gramática 1*

You are about to win a lot of money on a game show. Use the key to decipher the code on each balloon and find out how much money you would win if you chose that balloon. Write the amount on the line. Then, circle the balloon with the highest number to win the biggest prize.

Key:  = $100   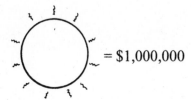 = $1,000   = $1,000,000

1. _____

2. _____

3. _____

4. _____

5. _____

6. _____

7. _____

8. _____

9. _____

10. _____

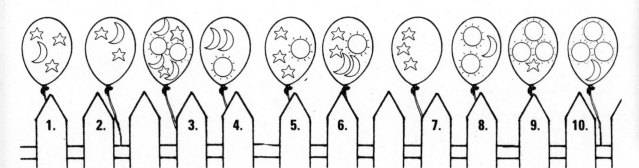

Which balloon do you choose? _____

La familia *Gramática en contexto*

Read the clues below to fill in the tree with the names of Flora and Diego's family members. Hints: Rectangles contain male family members and diamonds contain female family members. Two shapes touching are married couples. Arrows point to children. Straight lines connect brothers and sisters.

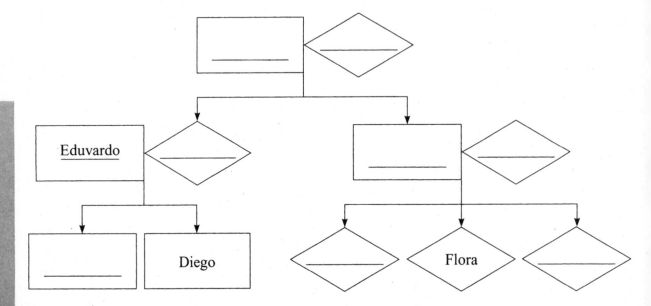

1. Flora es la hija de Cristina.

2. Ángela es la madre de José.

3. Antonio es el primo de Jamie.

4. Pilar es la hermana de Flora.

5. José es el tío de Diego.

6. Ronaldo es el abuelo de Antonio.

7. Diego es el hijo de Lisa.

8. Ángela es la abuela de Pilar.

9. Cristina es la tía de Diego.

10. José es el hermano de Lisa.

El desorden *Práctica de gramática 2*

In the middle of Spanish class, there was a fire drill. In the race to get out,
everybody's things were moved around. Now that you're back in the classroom, sort
out who has whose things using **mi(s), tu(s), su(s),** and **nuestro(a)(s).**

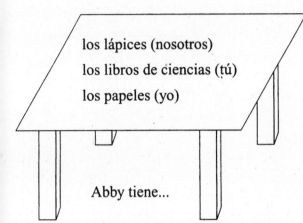

los lápices (nosotros)

los libros de ciencias (tú)

los papeles (yo)

Abby tiene...

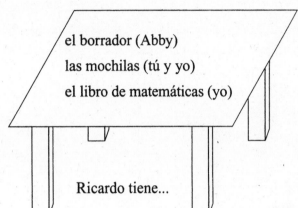

el borrador (Abby)

las mochilas (tú y yo)

el libro de matemáticas (yo)

Ricardo tiene...

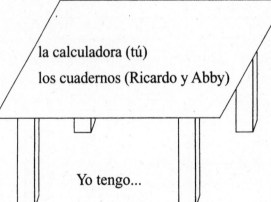

la calculadora (tú)

los cuadernos (Ricardo y Abby)

Yo tengo...

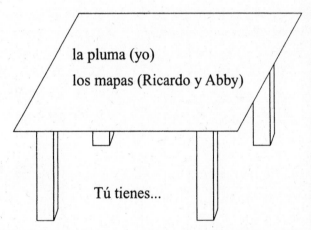

la pluma (yo)

los mapas (Ricardo y Abby)

Tú tienes...

1. _____

2. _____

3. _____

4. _____

Nombre _____ Clase _____ Fecha _____

El calendario *Todo junto*

Your calendar is scrambled! Use the key below to decode the names of the months.
Hint: use the number of days in the months to help you.

1. XRNIZN

_____

L	M	M	J	V	S	D
	1	2	3	4	5	6
7	8	9	10	11	12	13
14	15	16	17	18	19	20
21	22	23	24	25	26	27
28	29	30	31			

2. HXSN

_____

L	M	M	J	V	S	D
1	2	3	4	5	6	7
8	9	10	11	12	13	14
15	16	17	18	19	20	21
22	23	24	25	26	27	28
29	30	31				

3. HXGCN

_____

L	M	M	J	V	S	D
		1	2	3	4	5
6	7	8	9	10	11	12
13	14	15	16	17	18	19
20	21	22	23	24	25	26
27	28	29	30	31		

4. NKZVUGA

_____

L	M	M	J	V	S	D
						1
2	3	4	5	6	7	8
9	10	11	12	13	14	15
16	17	18	19	20	21	22
23/30	24/31	25	26	27	28	29

5. MPKPAHUGA

_____

L	M	M	J	V	S	D
				1	2	3
4	5	6	7	8	9	10
11	12	13	14	15	16	17
18	19	20	21	22	23	24
25	26	27	28	29	30	31

6. AQAGN

_____

L	M	M	J	V	S	D
						1
2	3	4	5	6	7	8
9	10	11	12	13	14	15
16	17	18	19	20	21	22
23/30	24/31	25	26	27	28	29

7. OVQPN

_____

L	M	M	J	V	S	D
		1	2	3	4	
5	6	7	8	9	10	11
12	13	14	15	16	17	18
19	20	21	22	23	24	25
26	27	28	29	30		

8. IABZPAHUGA

_____

L	M	M	J	V	S	D
				1	2	3
4	5	6	7	8	9	10
11	12	13	14	15	16	17
18	19	20	21	22	23	24
25	26	27	28	29	30	

9. QNWPAHUGA

_____

L	M	M	J	V	S	D
		1	2	3	4	5
6	7	8	9	10	11	12
13	14	15	16	17	18	19
20	21	22	23	24	25	26
27	28	29	30			

10. YAUGAGN

_____

L	M	M	J	V	S	D
	1	2	3	4	5	
6	7	8	9	10	11	12
13	14	15	16	17	18	19
20	21	22	23	24	25	26
27	28					

11. XUGPJ

_____

L	M	M	J	V	S	D
					1	2
3	4	5	6	7	8	9
10	11	12	13	14	15	16
17	18	19	20	21	22	23
24	25	26	27	28	29	30

12. OVJPN

_____

L	M	M	J	V	S	D
					1	2
3	4	5	6	7	8	9
10	11	12	13	14	15	16
17	18	19	20	21	22	23
24/31	25	26	27	28	29	30

A	B	C	D	E	F	G	H	I	J	K	L	M	N	O	P	Q	R	S	T	U	V	W	X	Y	Z
							M													*B*					

Nombre _____ Clase _____ Fecha _____

¿Cuál es la fecha? *Lectura cultural*

Read the clues below and write out the date using the format **Hoy es el...**

1. Mañana es la Navidad (*Christmas*).

   _____

2. En dos meses es el cinco de mayo.

   _____

3. En una semana es el Día de la Independencia (*Independence Day*).

   _____

4. En dos semanas es el Día de la Amistad (*Valentine's Day*).

   _____

5. En cinco meses es New Year's Eve.

   _____

6. El día después de mañana es Halloween.

   _____

7. En ocho meses es la fecha de tu nacimiento.

   _____

El cumpleaños de la abuela *Repaso*

Every year on grandma's birthday her family comes to visit. This year there is something wrong. Look at the picture and write sentences describing all of the things you find wrong.

1. _____

2. _____

3. _____

4. _____

5. _____

Practice Games Answers

PAGE 31

Práctica de vocabulario

1. yogur
2. leche
3. huevo
4. café
5. manzana
6. hamburguesa
7. bebida
8. sopa
9. pan
10. cereal

PAGE 32

Vocabulario en contexto

1. el huevo
2. el jugo de naranja
3. el yogur, la leche, la hamburguesa, el queso
4. el pan, el cereal
5. el jamón
6. la manzana

Bonus: 3

PAGE 33

Práctica de gramática 1

Plural nouns: manzanas, mañanas, naranjas, bananas

Singular nouns: café, leche, huevo, queso

PAGE 34

Gramática en contexto

1. A papá le gusta el café.
2. A mis hermanos les gustan las frutas.
3. A nosotros nos gustan los sándwiches.
4. A mi me gusta el cereal.
5. A ti te gusta la sopa.

Practice Games Answers

PAGE 35

Práctica de grámatica 2

1. desayuno y café
2. huevo y pan
3. uvas y yogur
4. hamburguesa horrible
5. comida y bebida

Bonus: comida rica

PAGE 36

Todo junto

Sopa; Hamburguesas; Manzanas; Refrescos; Jugos

PAGE 37

Lectura cultural

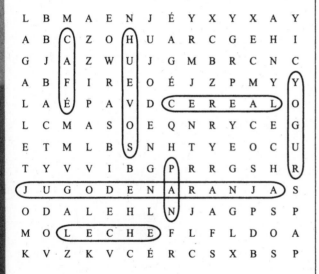

1. huevos
2. pan
3. cereal
4. café
5. leche
6. yogur
7. jugo de naranja

PAGE 38

Repaso

1. Carlos y Pablo tienen ganas de tocar la guitarra.
2. Ana tiene ganas de jugar al fútbol.
3. Marcos y yo tenemos ganas de beber café.
4. Isabel y tú tienen ganas de estudiar.
5. Paula tiene ganas de comer un sándwich.
6. Yo tengo ganas de mirar televisión.
7. Tu tienes ganas de comer una manzana.

Practice Games Answers

Práctica de vocabulario

Team Odd

1. Javier, 17
2. Papá, 37
3. Diana, 51
4. Celia, 45
5. Alejandro, 29
6. Abuelo, 63
7. Gregorio, 27

Team Even

1. Raúl, 14
2. Elisa, 20
3. Cristián, 34
4. Mamá, 38
5. Inés, 20
6. Melinda, 16
7. Juan, 32

PAGE 40

Vocabulario en contexto

1. mejor
2. más que
3. tanto como
4. mayor
5. menor
6. menos que

PAGE 41

Práctica de gramática 1

1. mil trescientos
2. mil doscientos
3. dos millón, tres mil doscientos
4. un millón dos mil
5. un millón trescientos
6. un millón dos mil doscientos
7. trescientos
8. dos millón mil
9. tres millón cien
10. tres millón mil

Balloon #10 is the biggest prize.

UNIDAD 3 Lección 2 Practice Games Answers

Practice Games Answers

PAGE 42

Gramática en contexto

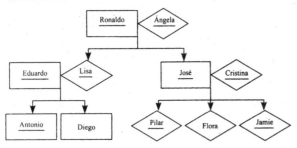

PAGE 43

Práctica de gramática 2

1. Abby tiene nuestros lápices, tus libros de ciencias y mis papeles.
2. Ricardo tiene su borrador, nuestras mochilas y mi libro de matemáticas.
3. Yo tengo tu calculadora y sus cuadernos.
4. Tú tienes mi pluma y sus mapas.

PAGE 44

Todo junto

1. agosto
2. mayo
3. marzo
4. octubre
5. diciembre
6. enero
7. junio
8. septiembre
9. noviembre
10. febrero
11. abril
12. julio

PAGE 45

Lectura cultural

1. Hoy es el veinticuatro de diciembre.
2. Hoy es el cinco de marzo.
3. Hoy es el veintisiete de junio.
4. Hoy es el primero de febrero.
5. Hoy es el treinta y uno de agosto.
6. Hoy es el veintinueve de octubre.
7. Answers will vary.

PAGE 46

Repaso

1. Febrero no tiene treinta días.
2. Es el cumpleaños de la abuela, no de los primos.
3. Abuela no tiene cuatrocientos años.
4. El perro come la comida del gato.
5. El pastel está debajo de la mesa.

Video Activities *Vocabulario*

PRE-VIEWING ACTIVITY

Before you view the video, answer these questions about food.

1. What are some of your favorite healthy foods?

_____

_____

2. What are some of your favorite junk foods?

_____

_____

3. What do you like to drink with meals?

_____

_____

4. What is your favorite meal of the day? Give an example of what you might eat for this meal.

_____

_____

VIEWING ACTIVITY

Read the list of foods below before you watch the video. Then, while you watch, indicate with a check (✓) whether the man at breakfast or the woman at lunch eats each food.

El hombre	La mujer		
_____	_____	**1.**	el café
_____	_____	**2.**	el cereal
_____	_____	**3.**	los huevos
_____	_____	**4.**	el jamón
_____	_____	**5.**	el jugo de naranja
_____	_____	**6.**	el pan
_____	_____	**7.**	el queso
_____	_____	**8.**	un sándwich
_____	_____	**9.**	la sopa
_____	_____	**10.**	el yogur

Video Activities *Vocabulario*

POST-VIEWING ACTIVITY

After viewing the video, list the foods in the word bank according to when they are eaten in the video.

| la banana | el café | el cereal | las hamburguesas | el jugo de naranja |
| los huevos | la leche | el pan | la sopa | el yogur | el sándwich |

EL DESAYUNO	EL ALMUERZO

LA CENA	EL BOCADO (*SNACK*)

52 Unidad 3, Lección 1
Video Activities

¡**Avancemos! 1**
Unit Resource Book

UNIDAD 3 Lección 1
Video Activities

Video Activities *Telehistoria escena 1*

PRE-VIEWING ACTIVITY

Answer the following questions.

1. Think of a time when you felt that someone was asking you too many questions. What did he or she want to know? How did the questions make you feel?

_____

_____

_____

2. Think of a time when you found yourself asking someone a lot of questions. How did the other person react? Did you find out what you wanted to know?

_____

_____

_____

3. Think of a situation in which asking many questions is important. Why do you think it is important to ask questions in this situation?

_____

_____

_____

_____

VIEWING ACTIVITY

Read the following list of activities before watching the video. While you watch the video, indicate with a checkmark (✓) which questions Marisol asks Rodrigo.

_____ **1.** ¿Por qué vas a la escuela hoy?

_____ **2.** ¿Qué clases tienes?

_____ **3.** ¿Cómo se llama?

_____ **4.** ¿Cómo es ella?

_____ **5.** ¿Cuándo tienes que estar en la escuela?

Video Activities *Telehistoria escena 1*

POST-VIEWING ACTIVITY

Choose the word(s) that best complete(s) each of the following sentences.

1. Rodrigo necesita _____ de Trini Salgado.

    a. una mochila

    b. un autógrafo

    c. una pluma

2. Rodrigo tiene _____ de Alicia.

    a. la camiseta

    b. el reloj

    c. la mochila

3. _____ de Rodrigo es de Miami.

    a. El libro

    b. El maestro

    c. La amiga

4. Trini Salgado llega a las _____ de la tarde.

    a. cinco

    b. dos

    c. cuatro

5. A Rodrigo no le gustan _____ .

    a. los deportes

    b. las preguntas

    c. las papas fritas

UNIDAD 3 Lección 1
Video Activities

Unidad 3, Lección 1
Video Activities

54

¡Avancemos! 1
Unit Resource Book

Video Activities *Telehistoria escena 2*

PRE-VIEWING ACTIVITY

Answer the following questions.

1. What are your favorite breakfast foods?

_____

_____

2. What do you normally have for breakfast?

_____

_____

3. What is nutritious about your breakfast? If nothing about it is nutritious, what could you do to make it healthier?

_____

_____

4. Do you consider breakfast to be an important meal? Why or why not?

_____

_____

VIEWING ACTIVITY

Read this activity before watching the video. Then, while you watch the video, indicate with a checkmark (✓) which foods Marisol and Rodrigo like to eat. There are some foods that neither of them like to eat.

	A Marisol le gusta(n)	A Rodrigo le gusta(n)
las bananas	_____	_____
el cereal	_____	_____
el yogur	_____	_____
las frutas	_____	_____
los huevos	_____	_____
las uvas	_____	_____
las manzanas	_____	_____
el pan	_____	_____
la leche	_____	_____
las galletas	_____	_____

Video Activities *Telehistoria escena 2*

POST-VIEWING ACTIVITY

Choose the word(s) that best complete(s) each of the following sentences.

hambre	pequeño	galletas	nutritiva	frutas

1. A Rodrigo le gusta comer comida _____ .

2. A Marisol le gusta un desayuno _____ .

3. Marisol tiene _____ porque no come mucho en el desayuno.

4. A Rodrigo le gustan las _____ .

5. A Marisol le gustan las _____ .

UNIDAD 3 Lección 1

Video Activities

56

Unidad 3, Lección 1
Video Activities

¡**Avancemos! 1**
Unit Resource Book

Video Activities *Telehistoria escena 3*

PRE-VIEWING ACTIVITY

Answer the following questions.

1. List five foods or drinks that are good for your health.

_____

2. List five foods or drinks that are bad for your health.

_____

3. Which foods and drinks listed in items 1 and 2 do you like?

_____

4. What is your typical daily menu like? Write what you eat for breakfast, lunch and dinner.

Breakfast: _____

Lunch: _____

Dinner: _____

VIEWING ACTIVITY

Read the following activity before watching the video. Then, while watching the video, indicate with a checkmark (✓) whether **Marisol** or **Rodrigo** says each of the following phrases. Hint: The phrases are reworded.

Marisol	**Rodrigo**	
_____	_____	**1.** ¿Comes helado para el almuerzo?
_____	_____	**2.** ¿Por qué no compartimos el helado?
_____	_____	**3.** Tengo ganas de comer papas fritas.
_____	_____	**4.** Necesitas comer comida nutritiva.
_____	_____	**5.** Me gusta comer comidas buenas de vez en cuando.
_____	_____	**6.** A mí me gustan los sándwiches de jamón y queso.

Video Activities *Telehistoria escena 3*

POST-VIEWING ACTIVITY

Indicate if each statement is true (T) or false (F).

1. Rodrigo come un sándwich para el almuerzo.   T   F

2. El helado es muy rico.   T   F

3. Marisol compra una hamburguesa con papas fritas.   T   F

4. Marisol bebe leche.   T   F

5. Cuando Marisol compra una bebida, Rodrigo come el helado.   T   F

6. Marisol tiene sed porque come un sándwich de jamón y queso.   T   F

7. Marisol come comidas buenas casi siempre.   T   F

8. Marisol tiene ganas de comer helado y papas fritas.   T   F

9. No venden papas fritas.   T   F

10. A Rodrigo le gusta el helado también.   T   F

Video Activities *Vocabulario*

PRE-VIEWING ACTIVITY

Answer the questions about family members before you watch the video.

1 Describe the members of your family or a friend's family.

_____

_____

2 How old is each person?

_____

_____

3 When are their birthdays?

_____

_____

4 What relatives do you enjoy visiting?

_____

_____

VIEWING ACTIVITY

Read the following list of Rodrigo's relatives before watching the video. While you watch, write **sí** (*yes*) next to the relatives who appear or are mentioned in the video. Write **no** (*no*) next to the people who do not appear and are not mentioned.

_____ **1.** la abuela

_____ **2.** el hermano Benito

_____ **3.** el hijo Roberto

_____ **4.** la madre

_____ **5.** el padre

_____ **6.** la madrastra

_____ **7.** el abuelo

_____ **8.** el primo Tito

_____ **9.** el tío Sergio

_____ **10.** la hermana Ana

_____ **11.** la prima Anita

_____ **12.** la tía Camila

_____ **13.** la prima Ester

_____ **14.** la tía Andrea

Video Activities *Vocabulario*

POST-VIEWING ACTIVITY

After you view the video, match each of Rodrigo's relatives to the correct description.

1. _____ Su cumpleaños es el 25 de febrero.

2. _____ Es la hermana menor del padre.

3. _____ Tiene setenta y cuatro años.

4. _____ Son los hijos de la tía.

5. _____ Tiene un hermano quien se llama Sergio.

6. _____ Es menor que Rodrigo.

a. los primos

b. el abuelo

c. la hermana Ana

d. la abuela

e. la tía Camila

f. el padre

UNIDAD 3 Lección 2

Video Activities

Unidad 3, Lección 2
Video Activities

60

¡Avancemos! 1
Unit Resource Book

Nombre _____ Clase _____ Fecha _____

Video Activities *Telehistoria escena 1*

PRE-VIEWING ACTIVITY

1. How did you celebrate your last birthday?

_____

_____

_____

2. Think of how someone younger or older than you celebrated his or her last birthday. How was the celebration different from yours?

_____

_____

_____

_____

3. What time of year is your birthday?

_____

_____

_____

VIEWING ACTIVITY

Indicate if each statement is true (T) or false (F).

1.	A Rodrigo no le gustan tostones.	T	F
2.	Hoy es el cumpleaños de la señora Vélez.	T	F
3.	Ana es la hermana menor de Rodrigo.	T	F
4.	La abuela de Marisol tiene ochenta años.	T	F
5.	La abuela de Marisol vive en Miami.	T	F
6.	El cumpleaños de Ana y la abuela de Marisol es el primero de marzo.	T	F
7.	La señora Vélez y su hija preparan la comida.	T	F

Video Activities *Telehistoria escena 1*

POST-VIEWING ACTIVITY

Match the appropriate answer to each of the following questions.

1. _____ ¿Mañana es el cumpleaños de la señora Vélez?

2. _____ ¿Cuántos años tiene Ana?

3. _____ ¿Cuándo es el cumpleaños de Ana?

4. _____ ¿Cuál es la fecha hoy?

5. _____ ¿Está Trini Salgado en la escuela hoy?

6. _____ ¿Dónde está la camiseta de Alicia?

a. Es el primero de marzo.

b. Sí. Está en el gimnasio a las cuatro.

c. Está encima del escritorio.

d. No. Es el cumpleaños de Ana.

e. Ella tiene nueve años.

f. Es el 28 de febrero.

62 Unidad 3, Lección 2
Video Activities

¡Avancemos! 1
Unit Resource Book

UNIDAD 3 Lección 2

Video Activities

Video Activities *Telehistoria escena 2*

PRE-VIEWING ACTIVITY

Fill in the blanks to complete these sentences about family relations.

1. Your female first cousin is your mother's _____ .

2. Your male first cousin is your grandfather's _____ .

3. Your grandparents are your uncle's _____ .

4. Your niece is your father's _____ .

VIEWING ACTIVITY

Read this activity before watching the video. While you watch the video, indicate with a checkmark (✓) what relation each of the following people has to Rodrigo.

	primo(a)	tío(a)	hermano(a)	madre
Señora Vélez	____	____	____	____
Camila	____	____	____	____
Ester	____	____	____	____
Tito	____	____	____	____
Inés	____	____	____	____
Mónica	____	____	____	____
Sergio	____	____	____	____

UNIDAD 3 Lección 2   Video Activities

Video Activities *Telehistoria escena 2*

POST-VIEWING ACTIVITY

Choose the word(s) that best complete(s) each of the following sentences.

1. Los primos de Rodrigo

    a. están en la casa de Rodrigo todos los viernes.

    b. están en la casa de Camila todos los viernes.

2. A los primos de Rodrigo

    a. les gusta comer pizza.

    b. les gusta practicar deportes.

3. La tía Camila

    a. tiene dos hijos.

    b. tiene dos hermanos.

4. Los primos Ester y Tito

    a. tienen trece y once años.

    b. tienen catorce y diez años.

5. Inés y Mónica

    a. son hermanas de la madre de Rodrigo.

    b. son hermanas del padre de Rodrigo.

6. El padre de Rodrigo

    a. tiene dos hermanos.

    b. tiene dos hermanas.

7. Tito

    a. tiene la camiseta de Alicia.

    b. no tiene la camiseta de Alicia.

8. A Tito

    a. le gustan mucho los refrescos.

    b. le gustan mucho los perros.

Video Activities *Telehistoria escena 3*

PRE-VIEWING ACTIVITY

Write your favorite and least favorite things in the following categories. Then, in complete sentences, compare the two things that you listed in each category. Give two comparisons for each category.

Category	Favorite	Least Favorite
1. Food	_____	_____
2. Drink	_____	_____
3. Music	_____	_____
4. Sport	_____	_____
5. Holiday	_____	_____

1. _____

_____

2. _____

_____

3. _____

_____

4. _____

_____

5. _____

VIEWING ACTIVITY

Read the following activity before watching the video. Then, while watching the video, indicate with a checkmark (✓) whether **Marisol** or **Rodrigo** says each of the following phrases.

Marisol	Rodrigo	
_____	_____	**1.** Tito es menor que tú, ¿no?
_____	_____	**2.** Los perros son simpáticos.
_____	_____	**3.** Los perros de Tito son muy grandes.
_____	_____	**4.** ¿Tiene Tito dos perros?
_____	_____	**5.** Sus perros son malos.
_____	_____	**6.** ¡Estás nerviosa!

Video Activities *Telehistoria escena 3*

POST-VIEWING ACTIVITY

Choose the correct word(s) to complete each of the following sentences.

1. **Rodrigo:** Tito es (menor / mayor) que yo.

2. **Marisol:** A mí me gustan (los gatos / los perros).

3. **Rodrigo:** Los gatos son más (simpáticos / perezosos) que los perros.

4. **Rodrigo:** A mí me gustan (los gatos / los perros).

5. **Marisol:** Los perros no son tan (simpáticos / perezosos) como los gatos.

6. **Rodrigo:** Los perros de Tito son tan (grandes / pequeños) como tú.

7. **Rodrigo:** Los perros son (peores / mejores) que los gatos.

8. **Rodrigo:** Tú estás más (desorganizada / nerviosa) que yo.

UNIDAD 3 Lección 2

Video Activities

Video Activities Answer Key

VOCABULARIO

PRE-VIEWING ACTIVITY p. 51

1. Answers will vary. I like pasta, cheese, tomatoes, and fruit.
2. Answers will vary. I enjoy potato chips and anything with chocolate.
3. Answers will vary. I like orange juice, water, or soda.
4. Answers will vary. Dinner is my favorite meal. I might have chicken, baked potatoes, broccoli, and water.

VIEWING ACTIVITY p. 51

1. la mujer	2. el hombre
3. el hombre	4. la mujer
5. el hombre	6. el hombre
7. la mujer	8. la mujer
9. la mujer	10. el hombre

POST-VIEWING ACTIVITY p. 52

EL DESAYUNO	EL ALMUERZO
los huevos	el sándwich
el cereal	el cafe
el pan	la leche
el yogur	el jugo de naranja

LA CENA	EL BOCADO (SNACK)
las hamburguesas	la banana
la sopa	

TELEHISTORIA ESCENA 1

PRE-VIEWING ACTIVITY p. 53

1. Answers will vary. Possible answer: I felt that my mother was asking me too many questions when I told her I was going out. She wanted to know exactly where I would be, who would be with me, and how long I would be there. It made me feel annoyed.
2. Answers will vary. Possible answer: I asked my friend a lot of questions when he said he was busy this weekend. I wanted to know if he was invited somewhere that I was not invited. He would not tell me whether or not he was.
3. Answers will vary. Possible answer: It is important to keep asking questions if you think that someone is doing something illegal or unsafe so that you can tell someone who can stop him or her.

VIEWING ACTIVITY p. 53

1. ¿Por qué vas tú a la escuela hoy? ✓
2. ¿Qué clase tienes?
3. ¿Cómo se llama? ✓
4. ¿Cómo es ella?
5. ¿Cuándo tienes que estar en la escuela? ✓

TELEHISTORIA ESCENA 1

POST-VIEWING ACTIVITY p. 54

1. b	2. a
3. c	4. c
5. b	

TELEHISTORIA ESCENA 2

PRE-VIEWING ACTIVITY p. 55

1. Answers will vary. Possible answer: My favorite breakfast foods are donuts, chocolate milk, and eggs with toast.
2. Answers will vary. Possible answer: I normally have cereal, a piece of toast, and a glass of orange juice for breakfast.
3. Answers will vary. Possible answer: My breakfast is nutritious. I eat a variety of healthy foods.
4. Answers will vary. Possible answer: Yes, I think breakfast is the most important meal of the day because it gives me energy to get started.

VIEWING ACTIVITY p. 55

Marisol: las galletas, Rodrigo: el cereal, el yogur, las frutas

POST-VIEWING ACTIVITY p. 56

1. nutritiva
2. pequeño
3. hambre
4. frutas
5. galletas

TELEHISTORIA ESCENA 3

PRE-VIEWING ACTIVITY p. 57

1. Answers will vary. Possible answers: chicken, grapes, yogurt, orange juice, bananas
2. Answers will vary. Possible answer: hamburgers, cookies, ice cream, soda, pizza

3. Answers will vary. Possible answer: I like yogurt, orange juice, cookies, ice cream, soda and pizza.
4. Answers will vary. Possible answer: Breakfast: cereal with milk and a piece of toast, Lunch: a turkey sandwich with potato chips and a soda, Dinner: spaghetti and meatballs

VIEWING ACTIVITY p. 57

1. Rodrigo
2. Marisol
3. Marisol
4. Rodrigo
5. Marisol
6. Marisol

POST-VIEWING ACTIVITY p. 58

1. T	2. T
3. F	4. F
5. T	6. F
7. F	8. F
9. T	10. T

UNIDAD 3 Lección 1   Video Activities Answer Key

Video Activities Answer Key

VOCABULARIO

PRE-VIEWING ACTIVITY p. 59

1. Answers will vary. Possible answer: I live with my mother, my father, and my younger sister.
2. Answers will vary. Possible answer: My mother is fifty-two, my father is fifty-four, and my sister is seventeen.
3. Answers will vary. Possible answer: My mother's birthday is August 24, my father's is May 22, and my sister's is May 18.
4. Answers will vary. Possible answer: I enjoy spending time with my grandparents.

VIEWING ACTIVITY p. 59

1. sí	**2.** no	**3.** no
4. sí	**5.** sí	**6.** no
7. sí	**8.** sí	**9.** sí
10. sí	**11.** no	**12.** sí
13. sí	**14.** no	

POST-VIEWING ACTIVITY p. 60

1. b	**2.** e	**3.** d
4. a	**5.** f	**6.** c

TELEHISTORIA ESCENA 1

PRE-VIEWING ACTIVITY p. 61

1. Answers will vary. Possible answer: I went out for pizza with my friends and then my parents gave me gifts.
2. Answers will vary. Possible answer: My younger sister celebrated her birthday by having a party with cake and ice cream. It was different from my birthday because birthdays are more exciting occasions for young children.
3. Answers will vary. Possible answer: My birthday is in the fall.

VIEWING ACTIVITY p. 61

1. F	**2.** F	**3.** T
4. F	**5.** T	**6.** T
7. F		

POST-VIEWING ACTIVITY p. 62

1. d	**2.** e	**3.** a
4. f	**5.** b	**6.** c

TELEHISTORIA ESCENA 2

PRE-VIEWING ACTIVITY p. 63

1. niece	**2.** grandson
3. parents	**4.** granddaughter

VIEWING ACTIVITY p. 63

Señora Vélez: madre

Camila: tía

Ester: prima

Tito : primo

Inés : tía

Mónica: tía

Sergio: tío

POST-VIEWING ACTIVITY p. 64

1. a	**2.** b	**3.** a
4. b	**5.** a	**6.** a
7. a	**8.** b	

TELEHISTORIA ESCENA 3

PRE-VIEWING ACTIVITY p. 65

1. Answers will vary. Possible answer: Pizza is tastier than cauliflower. Pizza is not as healthy as cauliflower.
2. Answers will vary. Possible answer: Milk isn't as sweet as soda and it is better for you.
3. Answers will vary. Possible answer: Hip-hop has a better beat than country music does. The lyrics in country music are better than the lyrics in hip hop.
4. Answers will vary. Possible answer: Swimming is more fun than volleyball. You use your feet more in soccer than you do in volleyball.
5. Answers will vary. Possible answer: Halloween is more interesting than Easter. I get to do more things on Halloween than I do on Easter.

VIEWING ACTIVITY p. 65

1. Marisol
2. Marisol
3. Rodrigo
4. Marisol
5. Rodrigo
6. Rodrigo

POST-VIEWING ACTIVITY p. 66

1. menor
2. los perros
3. simpáticos
4. los gatos
5. perezosos
6. grandes
7. peores
8. nerviosa

Video Scripts

VOCABULARIO

Rodrigo: Hola. Soy Rodrigo.

Marisol: Y yo soy Marisol.

Rodrigo: ¿Tienes ganas de comer? Tenemos mucha comida buena.

Marisol: ¿Qué le gusta comer en el desayuno?

Rodrigo: Los huevos.

Marisol: El cereal.

Rodrigo: El pan.

Marisol: Y el yogur.

Rodrigo: ¿Una bebida?

Hombre: Sí, por favor. Un jugo de manzana. Gracias.

Marisol: ¡Ah! ¡El almuerzo!

Rodrigo: ¿Qué es?

Mujer: Un sándwich de jamón y queso.

Marisol: Ummm... ¿bueno?

Mujer: Sí, muy rico. Pero tengo sed.

Rodrigo: ¿Una bebida?

Mujer: Un café, por favor.

Marisol: ¿Con leche?

Mujer: Sí, gracias.

Marisol: Es la hora de la cena.

Rodrigo: Una hamburguesa.

Marisol: Y una sopa.

Mujer 2: La sopa es horrible.

Marisol: ¿Horrible?

Mujer 2: No, es muy rica.

Marisol: ¡Ah, qué bueno!

Rodrigo: ¿Tienes hambre?

Marisol: Sí, tengo mucha hambre.

Rodrigo: ¡Las galletas no son nutritivas! ¿Unas uvas? ¿Una manzana? ¿Una banana, o como decimos en Puerto Rico, un guineo?

Marisol: Unas uvas, por favor. ¿Tienes ganas de comer unas uvas?

Rodrigo: ¡Sí!

Marisol: ¿Compartimos?

Rodrigo: ¡Bueno!

TELEHISTORIA ESCENA 1

Marisol: ¿A la escuela? ¿Por qué vas a la escuela hoy? Es sábado.

Rodrigo: Trini Salgado llega hoy y necesito un autógrafo... en una camiseta. Es importante.

Marisol: ¿En una camiseta? ¿Qué camiseta?

Rodrigo: Tengo una amiga...

Marisol: ¿Una amiga? ¿Qué amiga? ¿Cómo se llama?

Rodrigo: Se llama Alicia.

Marisol: ¿Alicia? ¿Y quién es Alicia?

Rodrigo: Ella no es de San Juan.

Marisol: ¿De dónde es?

Rodrigo: Es de Miami.

Marisol: ¿Cuándo tienes que estar en la escuela?

Rodrigo: A las 4 de la tarde. ¡Y por favor! ¡No más preguntas!

Marisol: Quince, veinte, cuarenta.

Video Scripts

TELEHISTORIA ESCENA 2

Rodrigo: Para el desayuno, mañana.

Marisol: ¿Qué te gusta comer en el desayuno?

Rodrigo: Me gusta el cereal, el yogur, las frutas. Y a ti, Marisol, ¿qué te gusta comer en el desayuno?

Marisol: No me gusta el yogur, y no me gustan los huevos.

Rodrigo: ¿Te gustan las frutas? ¿Las uvas, las manzanas?

Marisol: No me gusta comer mucho en el desayuno.

Rodrigo: ¡Tienes que comer bien en el desayuno! ¿Te gusta el pan? ¿O la leche?

Marisol: Me gustan las galletas. Tengo hambre.

Rodrigo: ¡Sí, tienes hambre! ¡Porque no te gusta comer mucho en el desayuno!

TELEHISTORIA ESCENA 3

Rodrigo: ¿Helado? ¿En el almuerzo?

Marisol: Sí, tengo ganas de comer helado. ¿Compartimos?

Rodrigo: El helado no es nutritivo.

Marisol: ¡Pero es muy rico!

Rodrigo: ¿Qué comes en la cena? ¿Una hamburguesa con papas fritas?

Marisol: Uhh... ¿Venden papas fritas?

Rodrigo: Tienes que comer comidas buenas.

Marisol: Sí, sí, yo como comida nutritiva de vez en cuando.

Rodrigo: ¿Sí? ¿Qué comes?

Marisol: Me gusta la sopa.

Rodrigo: La sopa es muy buena.

Marisol: Me gustan los sándwiches de jamón y queso. Pero ahora tengo sed. Necesito una bebida.

Rodrigo: El helado es muy rico.

Video Scripts

VOCABULARIO

Rodrigo: Marisol, ella es mi madre.

Marisol: Mucho gusto.

Madre: Rodrigo, ¿qué fecha es hoy?

Rodrigo: Es el 25 de febrero.

Madre: ¡Es el cumpleaños de tu abuelo!

Marisol: ¿Ellos son tus abuelos?

Rodrigo: Sí. El es mi abuelo Cristóbal y mi abuela María.

Marisol: ¿Y cuántos años tienen?

Rodrigo: ¿Ciento cincuenta?

Madre: ¡Rodrigo! No, no. La abuela tiene setenta y cuatro años y el abuelo tiene setenta y seis.

Rodrigo: Setenta y cuatro y setenta y seis... ¡Ciento cincuenta!

Marisol: ¿Son sus padres?

Madre: No, son los padres del padre de Rodrigo. Él es el padre de Rodrigo, su hermano Sergio y su hermana Camila.

Rodrigo: Mi tío Sergio es mayor que mi padre y mí tía Camila es menor.

Marisol: ¿Tienes primos?

Rodrigo: Ellos son mis primos. Hijos de tía Camila: mi primo Tito y mi prima Ester, ...y su gata Princesa.

Marisol: ¡Qué simpáticos!

Rodrigo: Es mi hermana Ana. Es menor que yo.

Madre: Es el 25 de diciembre de 1996. El cumpleaños de Rodrigo, el primero de abril.

Rodrigo: Tengo que hablar con mi abuelo. Abuelo, ¡feliz cumpleaños! Sí.

TELEHISTORIA ESCENA 1

Rodrigo: Hola, mamá.

Madre: ¡Hola!

Marisol: ¡Hola!

Madre: ¡Hola!

Ana: ¡Hola!

Rodrigo: Mmmmm... ¡Tostones! ¡Qué rico!...

Marisol: Hola, señora Vélez. ¡Ah! ¿Es su cumpleaños? Hi, Mrs. Velez.

Madre: No, es el cumpleaños de Ana.

Rodrigo: Mi hermana pequeña ahora es grande.

Marisol: ¡Feliz cumpleaños! ¿Cuántos años tienes?

Ana: Hoy tengo nueve años. ¡Mañana, diez!

Marisol: ¿Mañana? ¿El 28 de febrero?

Rodrigo: No. El primero de marzo.

Marisol: El cumpleaños de mi abuela es el primero de marzo. Ella vive en Miami.

Ana: ¿Ah sí? ¿Cuántos años tiene?

Marisol: Tiene sesenta y ocho años.

Rodrigo: Mamá, ¿dónde está la camiseta?

Madre: ¿La camiseta de Alicia?

Rodrigo: Sí. Trini Salgado está en la escuela a las cuatro.

Madre: Está encima del escritorio.

TELEHISTORIA ESCENA 2

Rodrigo: No, no está. ¿Dónde está la camiseta?

Madre: ¡Tus primos!

Marisol: ¿Tus primos tienen la camiseta de Alicia?

Rodrigo: Ellos comen con nosotros todos los viernes. A nuestros primos les gusta jugar al fútbol, y es una camiseta del Club Atlético Palmeras.

Madre: ¿Camila? Es Celia. Tengo una pregunta.

Rodrigo: Es mi tía Camila. La tía Camila es la madre de Ester y Tito. Mis primos tienen catorce y diez años.

Marisol: ¿Es tu familia?

Rodrigo: Mi madre tiene dos hermanas: Inés y Mónica. Mi padre tiene un hermano, Sergio, y una hermana, Camila.

Madre: ¡Gracias! Rodrigo, tu primo Tito tiene la camiseta de tu amiga Alicia.

Marisol: ¡Ay, qué bueno! ¿no?

Rodrigo: Mi primo tiene perros muy grandes. No me gustan los perros de Tito.

Video Scripts

TELEHISTORIA ESCENA 3

Marisol: Tu primo, Tito, ¿es menor que tú?

Rodrigo: Sí, pero...

Marisol: ¿Qué?

Rodrigo: Sus perros. No me gustan sus perros.

Marisol: ¿No te gustan los perros? Son simpáticos.

Rodrigo: Me gustan más los gatos. Son más simpáticos que los perros.

Marisol: Los perros son menos perezosos que los gatos.

Rodrigo: Los perros de Tito son perezosos y muy grandes. ¡Son tan grandes como tú!

Marisol: ¿Cúantos perros tiene? ¿Dos?

Rodrigo: No, tiene más de dos. Sus perros son muy malos. Y peores que los gatos.

Marisol: Rodrigo, ¡No hay perros!

Rodrigo: ¡Sí, hay perros! ¡Estás tan nerviosa como yo!

Marisol: Peor.

Rodrigo: ¡Tito! ¡Tito!

Tito: ¡Hola, Rodrigo! Tu camiseta.

LEVEL 1 UNIT 3 CULTURE SEGMENT

FOOD—PUERTO RICO

Puerto Rico

Foods across the Spanish-speaking world vary from one another. Here we are going to show you a refreshing Puerto Rican treat, an interesting place dedicated to ham in Spain, and a street grill in Argentina.

In Puerto Rico there is no day at the beach without a pan of homemade rice, or a BBQ.

And for those who don't bring their own food, there are always plenty of stands that sell traditional fried snacks made with plantain and seafood.

In Puerto Rico this is a very common sound in plazas. This man is making a **piragua**, or a shaved ice cone, a traditional Puerto Rican treat. Raspberry, coconut, and lemon are popular flavors, but for more adventurous eaters there is also tamarind and guava.

Spain

The Spanish love for ham is evident in the **Museo del Jamón**, an interesting place where you can sample many different varieties of ham from all over the country, such as Iberian acorn ham, made from black hogs fed with a blend of herbs and acorns.

Spain is also known for the Spanish tortilla, a delicious egg dish made with potatoes and onions, that is a staple of Spanish cuisine...and for their delicious seafood, that is often seasoned with olive oil, peppers, and black olives.

Argentina

In Argentina they love beef. You can find a street grill on almost every other corner in Buenos Aires. In a typical Argentinean grill you will see many different cuts of meat. Argentina is definitely a place for meat-lovers.

As we have seen here, food across the Spanish-speaking world is very different, and there are many delicious things to choose from. **¡Buen provecho!**

Audio Scripts

PRESENTACIÓN DE VOCABULARIO

Level 1 Textbook pp. 140-141
Level 1A Textbook pp. 156-158
TXT CD 3, Track 1

A. ¡Hola! Me llamo Rodrigo y ella es Ana. Son las ocho de la mañana. Es importante comer un desayuno nutritivo todos los días.

B. Cuando tengo hambre, me gusta comer huevos y pan. Cuando tengo sed, bebo jugo de naranja. Me gusta mucho porque es rico. Nunca bebo café porque es horrible.

C. Es la una y ahora Marisol y yo comemos el almuerzo. En la cafetería venden muchas comidas: sándwiches, hamburguesas y sopa. También venden bebidas: leche, jugos y refrescos.

D. Marisol y yo compramos fruta para mi papá: manzanas, bananas y uvas. La cena es a las siete y tengo ganas de comer. Siempre como mucho cuando mi mamá prepara la comida.

Narrator: En Puerto Rico se dice...

In Puerto Rico the word for orange juice is *el jugo de china*. The word for banana is *el guineo*.

¡A RESPONDER!

Level 1 Textbook p. 141
Level 1A Textbook p. 158
TXT CD 3, Track 2

Write **desayuno** and **almuerzo** on separate pieces of paper. Listen to the list of foods. Hold up the correct piece or pieces of paper to indicate when you eat each food.

1. la hamburguesa

2. la leche

3. el pan

4. el sándwich de jamón y queso

5. el cereal

6. la sopa

7. el huevo

8. el café

TELEHISTORIA ESCENA 1

Level 1 Textbook p. 143
Level 1A Textbook p. 160
TXT CD 3, Track 3

Marisol: ¿A la escuela? ¿Por qué vas a la escuela hoy? Es sábado.

Rodrigo: Trini Salgado llega hoy y necesito un autógrafo en una camiseta. Es importante.

Marisol: ¿En una camiseta? ¿Qué camiseta?

Rodrigo: Tengo una amiga...

Marisol: ¿Una amiga? ¿Qué amiga? ¿Cómo se llama?

Rodrigo: Se llama Alicia.

Marisol: ¿De dónde es?

Rodrigo: Es de Miami.

Marisol: ¿Cuándo tienes que estar en la escuela?

Rodrigo: A las cuatro de la tarde. ¡Y por favor! ¡No más preguntas!

Marisol: Quince, veinte, cuarenta...

PRONUNCIACIÓN

Level 1 Textbook p. 146
Level 1A Textbook p. 163
TXT CD 3, Track 4

Las letras **r** y **rr**

In Spanish, the letter **r** in the middle or the end of a word is pronounced by a single tap of the tongue against the gum above the upper front teeth. The letter **r** at the beginning of a word or **rr** within a word is pronounced by several rapid taps called a trill. Listen and repeat.

para
cereal
beber
yogur
rico
rubio
horrible
pizarrón

El cereal y el yogur son ricos; no son horribles.

TELEHISTORIA ESCENA 2

Level 1 Textbook p. 148
Level 1A Textbook p. 166
TXT CD 3, Track 5

Marisol: ¿Qué te gusta comer en el desayuno?

Rodrigo: Me gustan el cereal, el yogur, las frutas. Y a ti, Marisol, ¿qué te gusta comer en el desayuno?

Marisol: No me gusta el yogur y no me gustan los huevos.

Rodrigo: ¿Te gustan las frutas? ¿Las uvas, las manzanas?

Marisol: No me gusta comer mucho en el desayuno.

Rodrigo: ¡Tienes que comer bien en el desayuno! ¿Te gusta el pan? ¿O la leche?

Marisol: Me gustan las galletas. Tengo hambre.

Rodrigo: Sí. ¡Porque no te gusta comer mucho en el desayuno!

ACTIVIDAD 15 (17) – ACTIVIDADES EN EL ALMUERZO

Level 1 Textbook p. 151
Level 1A Textbook, Act. p. 169
TXT CD 3, Track 6

Listen to the descriptions of Marisol and her friends, and take notes. Then write sentences saying who does what, using elements from each puzzle piece.

Marisol: ¡Hola! Soy Marisol. Antes del almuerzo, tengo la clase de inglés. Escribo en el cuaderno, pero es difícil porque tengo mucha hambre.

Rodrigo: Soy Rodrigo. Es la hora del almuerzo. Hmmm... la cafetería vende sopa, uvas y bananas.

Mateo: Me llamo Mateo. ¡Me gusta la comida nutritiva! Hoy Rodrigo y yo comemos uvas.

Carmen: Hola, me llamo Carmen. Ahora estoy en la cafetería. Bebo jugo de naranja porque tengo sed. ¡Es rico!

Carmen: Raúl y David, ¿qué hacen ustedes? ¿Por qué no comen?

Audio Scripts

Raúl: Leemos un libro. Nos gustan los libros.

Laura: Hola, soy Laura. Hoy la cafetería no vende sándwiches. ¡Qué horrible! Pero mi amiga Diana tiene un sándwich y nosotras compartimos. Es una buena amiga.

TELEHISTORIA COMPLETA

Level 1 Textbook p. 153

Level 1A Textbook p. 172

TXT CD 3, Track 7

Escena 1 - Resumen

Rodrigo necesita el autógrafo de Trini Salgado para Alicia. Tiene que estar en la escuela a las cuatro de la tarde.

Escena 2 - Resumen

Rodrigo compra comida. Le gusta la comida nutritiva. Marisol tiene hambre porque no le gusta comer mucho en el desayuno.

Escena 3

Rodrigo: ¿Helado? ¿En el almuerzo?

Marisol: Sí, tengo ganas de comer helado. ¿Compartimos?

Rodrigo: El helado no es nutritivo.

Marisol: ¡Pero es muy rico!

Rodrigo: ¿Qué comes en la cena? ¿Una hamburguesa con papas fritas?

Marisol: ¿Venden papas fritas?

Rodrigo: Tienes que comer comidas buenas.

Marisol: Sí, sí. Yo como comida nutritiva de vez en cuando.

Rodrigo: ¿Sí? ¿Qué comes?

Marisol: Me gusta la sopa.

Rodrigo: La sopa es muy buena.

Marisol: Necesito una bebida.

Rodrigo: El helado es muy rico.

ACTIVIDAD 20 (24) – INTEGRACIÓN

Level 1 Textbook p. 155

Level 1A Textbook, Act. 24 p. 174

TXT CD 3, Track 8

Read the newspaper ad for Supermercado Grande. Then listen to the radio ad for Supermercado Econo. Say what foods you like and where they sell them.

FUENTE 2 ANUNCIO DE RADIO

TXT CD 3, Track 9

Listen and take notes.

¿Qué comidas venden en el Supermercado Econo?

¿Qué venden en la cafetería?

Announcer: ¿Tienes hambre? En Supermercado Econo vendemos todo para el desayuno: cereal, huevos y muchas frutas. También hay almuerzo todos los días en la cafetería dentro del supermercado. Vendemos hamburguesas muy ricas, sándwiches de jamón, sopas nutritivas y ¡más!

LECTURA: ¡A COMPRAR Y A COMER!

Level 1 Textbook pp. 156-157

Level 1A Textbook pp. 176-177

TXT CD 3, Track 10

The following is a supermarket circular from Supermercados La Famosa and a shopping list.

Supermercados La Famosa.
Tenemos buenos precios y productos superiores

Hamburguesas El bohío, 1.5 lbs., $1.29

Queso americano de sándwich Vitarroz, 12 oz., $1.79

Jamón de sándwich Astor, $1.79/lb.

Uvas de California, $1.59/lb.

Yogur de mango La Yogúrt, 59¢

Queso crema La Cremosa, 8 oz., $1.29

Leche condensada La Fe, 14 oz., 99¢

Huevos del país, $1.19

Jamón ovalado Hak, 5 lbs., $9.99

Manzanas rojas, 79¢/lb

Jugo de china, Valemil, 64 oz., $2.69

Jugo de piña Tropical, de concentrado, 12 oz., 99 ¢

Pan de sándwich Club, 24 oz., $1.69

Pan Criollo, 1 lb., $1.29

Café El Morro, 16 oz., $3.49

Precios válidos el viernes, el sábado y el domingo

Lista de compras
café

huevos
leche condensada
jugo de china
pan
yogur
cereal
jamón de sándwich
queso de sándwich
uvas
manzanas

REPASO: ACTIVIDAD 1 – LISTEN AND UNDERSTAND

Level 1 Textbook p. 160

Level 1A Textbook p. 180

TXT CD 3, Track 11

Lola never eats traditional meals. Listen to the radio interview. Write **el desayuno**, **el almuerzo**, or **la cena**, according to when she eats or drinks each item.

Roque: Gracias por estar con nosotros, Lola.

Lola: El gusto es mío, Roque. Me gusta hablar de la comida.

Roque: Ah, ¿sí? ¿Qué te gusta comer más?

Lola: Las hamburguesas son muy ricas. En el desayuno como dos hamburguesas casi todos los días.

Roque: ¿Te gustan las hamburguesas en el desayuno? Interesante. ¿Y bebes café también?

Lola: No, el café es para la cena. Bebo café todas las noches.

Roque: ¿Qué te gusta comer en la cena?

Lola: Siempre como huevos y pan.

Roque: ¿Qué comes y bebes en el almuerzo?

Lola: Como cereal y una banana.

Roque: ¿Bebes leche?

Lola: Sí, bebo leche en el almuerzo porque es muy buena.

Roque: También bebes leche en el desayuno, ¿no?

Audio Scripts

Lola: No, me gusta más beber un refresco en el desayuno.

Roque: Gracias, Lola. Eres una persona muy interesante.

WORKBOOK SCRIPTS
WB CD 2

INTEGRACIÓN HABLAR

Level 1 Workbook p. 108
Level 1A Workbook p. 110
WB CD 2, Track 1

Listen to Alejandro's voicemail message for "El Sándwich Divertido." Take notes.

FUENTE 2

WB CD 2, Track 2

¡Hola! Soy Alejandro. Mis amigos y yo trabajamos cerca de "El Sándwich Divertido". Siempre tengo mucha hambre para el almuerzo. Pero no me gustan las hamburguesas ni las papas fritas. Son horribles. Me gusta comer muy bien, porque soy atlético. Bebo jugo y no me gustan los refrescos. No son nutritivos. Para el almuerzo, tengo ganas de comer...

INTEGRACIÓN ESCRIBIR

Level 1 Workbook p. 109
Level 1A Workbook p. 111
WB CD 2, Track 3

Listen to the voicemail message that Ramón's mother left on his answering machine. Take notes.

FUENTE 2

WB CD 2, Track 4

¡Hola, Ramón! Estoy en la oficina. Mañana tienes mucha comida para un desayuno nutritivo. No hay jugo de naranja pero sí hay un jugo de uvas muy rico. También hay cereal y leche. No hay manzanas pero hay tres bananas. Tienes que preparar un desayuno nutritivo con la comida que hay. ¡Nada de comer galletas temprano en la mañana! Hablamos en la tarde.

ESCUCHAR A, ACTIVIDAD 1

Level 1 Workbook p. 110
Level 1A Workbook p. 112
WB CD 2, Track 5

Listen to Carla and take notes. Then read each sentence and answer cierto (true) or falso (false).

Carla: Hola, me llamo Carla. A mí me gusta la comida nutritiva. Siempre como frutas, huevos o yogur. También bebo leche o jugo de frutas. A mi amiga Elena no le gusta la comida nutritiva. En el desayuno, ella come pizza o galletas y bebe refrescos. La comida de Elena no es buena.

ESCUCHAR A, ACTIVIDAD 2

Level 1 Workbook p. 110
Level 1A Workbook p. 112
WB CD 2, Track 6

Listen to Natalia and take notes. Then, complete the sentences below.

Natalia: Buenos días, me llamo Natalia. Hoy, mis amigos y yo comemos en la cafetería. En la cafetería siempre venden comida nutritiva. A nosotros nos gustan mucho los sándwiches y la sopa. Bebemos jugo de naranja o agua. Mi amiga Amalia nunca come en la cafetería. A ella no le gusta la comida nutritiva.

ESCUCHAR B, ACTIVIDAD 1

Level 1 Workbook p. 111
Level 1A Workbook p. 113
WB CD 2, Track 7

Listen to Andrés and take notes. Then complete the following sentences.

Andrés: Hola, soy Andrés. Mi papá siempre prepara el desayuno para la familia. Mi papá come huevos y pan, y bebe jugo de naranja todos los días. A mí me gusta más el cereal pero también bebo jugo de naranja. Mi mamá come yogur con frutas todas las mañanas y bebe café. Muchas veces, cuando hay bananas, mi mamá y yo compartimos.

ESCUCHAR B, ACTIVIDAD 2

Level 1 Workbook p. 111
Level 1A Workbook p. 113
WB CD 2, Track 8

Listen to Mrs. Márquez. Then answer the questions below in complete sentences.

Sra. Márquez: Buenos días, soy la señora Márquez. A todos en casa les gustan las comidas que hago para el desayuno. A Verónica y al papá les gusta el jugo de naranja. Yo bebo leche y también me gusta el café. Como frutas y el cereal. Andrea y su papá comen huevos. Muchas veces comparto unas frutas con Andrea. A ella le gustan mucho las uvas y manzanas.

ESCUCHAR C, ACTIVIDAD 1

Level 1 Workbook p. 112
Level 1A Workbook p. 114
WB CD 2, Track 9

Listen to Lucía talk about her food. Take notes. Then list the foods she likes and does not like.

Lucía: Me llamo Lucía. Nunca bebo café. Es horrible. A mí me gustan la leche y el yogur. Son muy ricos. También me gustan los sándwiches de queso, pero nunca como los sándwiches de jamón. No me gustan. Siempre como frutas. Me gustan las bananas y las manzanas, pero no me gustan las naranjas. No me gustan las uvas. Nunca como uvas y nunca como sopa. No me gusta la sopa.

ESCUCHAR C, ACTIVIDAD 2

Level 1 Workbook p. 112
Level 1A Workbook p. 114
WB CD 2, Track 10

Listen to Santiago and take notes. Then, in complete sentences, answer the questions about what they like.

Santiago: Me llamo Santiago y mi amiga es Ana. Ana nunca bebe refrescos, pero a mí me gustan mucho. ¡Son muy ricos! Ana come cereal y huevos. Me gusta el cereal pero no me gustan los huevos. Ana come sándwiches de queso pero nunca come jamón. A mí me gustan todos los sándwiches. Muchas veces comparto un sándwich de queso con ella.

Audio Scripts

ASSESSMENT SCRIPTS
TEST CD 1

LESSON 1 TEST: ESCUCHAR ACTIVIDAD A

Modified Assessment Book p. 83
On-level Assessment Book p. 108
Pre-AP Assessment Book p. 83
TEST CD 1, Track 15

Narrador: Listen to the following audio. Then complete Activity A.

Sra. Rodríguez: Tengo ganas de comer algo nutritivo. ¿Por qué no comemos una sopa con una ensalada?

Sr. Rodríguez: A mí no me gusta la ensalada. ¿Por qué no comemos hamburguesas? Tengo mucha hambre y me gustan mucho las hamburguesas.

Sra. Rodríguez: A mí no me gustan las hamburguesas. ¿Comemos fruta? Tengo ganas de hacer una ensalada de fruta. ¿Te gusta comer frutas?

Sr. Rodríguez: Sí, me gustan mucho las uvas y las bananas.

Sra. Rodríguez: A mí también me gustan las uvas pero no me gustan las bananas. Me gustan mucho las manzanas.

Sr. Rodríguez: Tengo mucha sed.

Sra. Rodríguez: ¿Qué te gusta beber?

Sr. Rodríguez: Me gusta el jugo de naranja.

Sra. Rodríguez: A mí también me gusta el jugo de naranja.

LESSON 1 TEST: ESCUCHAR ACTIVIDAD B

Modified Assessment Book p. 83
On-level Assessment Book p. 108
Pre-AP Assessment Book p. 83
TEST CD 1, Track 16

Narradora: Listen to the following audio. Then complete Activity B.

Hotel employee: Buenos días.

Señora Contreras: Buenos días. Hoy tengo mucha hambre. Tengo ganas de comer un desayuno nutritivo. Me gusta el cereal con leche. También me gusta comer huevos. Pero no me gusta el pan. No tengo ganas de comer pan con los huevos. Para beber me gusta el jugo de naranja, por favor. Y para comer, una fruta.... una manzana, por favor. Muchas gracias.

UNIDAD 3, LECCIÓN 1
HL CDS 1 & 3

INTEGRACIÓN HABLAR

Level 1 HL Workbook p. 110
Level 1A HL Workbook p. 112
HL CD 1, Track 17

Escucha el siguiente fragmento de un programa de radio. Toma notas.

FUENTE 2

HL CD 1, Track 18

La sopa de pasta es muy fácil de preparar. No se preocupe. Caliente agua con sal, pimienta, mucho cilantro y un trozo grande de carne para hacer un buen caldo. Mientras se cocina todo esto, pele cuatro papas, córtelas en trocitos y póngalas en el agua para que se ablanden. Corte también cuatro zanahorias y un poco de apio y agréguelos al caldo. Cuando todo esté blandito, agregue media libra de pasta y revuelva bien. Déjelo cocinar hasta que la pasta se ablande. Sirva la sopa bien caliente, acompañada con pan. También puede usar un poco de picante. ¡Queda deliciosa!

INTEGRACIÓN ESCRIBIR

Level 1 Workbook p. 111
Level 1A HL Workbook p. 113
HL CD 1, Track 19

Escucha parte de una entrevista que hizo una estación de radio a una mujer puertorriqueña. Toma notas.

FUENTE 2

HL CD 1, Track 20

Los desayunos que más recuerdo son los de mi abuela. Como no me gustaban los huevos, ella me preparaba muchas cosas riquísimas: pan con miel, jugo, cereal y jamón. También me gustaba mucho comer unos panecillos dulces de huevo que se remojaban en el chocolate caliente. Para el almuerzo, mi mamá nos preparaba algo delicioso y nutritivo. Nada de pizza ni papas fritas. Con frecuencia nos daba pollo asado. Y casi siempre había arroz y ensalada. El dulce de guayaba era mi postre favorito. Pero no me haga hablar de comida, que ya tengo hambre y son apenas las once de la mañana.

LESSON 1 TEST: ESCUCHAR, ACTIVIDAD A

HL Assessment Book p. 89
HL CD 3, Track 15

Escucha una conversación entre dos hermanos, Miguel y Sara. A los dos les gustan diferentes comidas y bebidas. Luego contesta las siguientes preguntas con oraciones completas.

Miguel: Tengo ganas de comer una hamburguesa, con unas papas fritas.

Sara: ¡No! Yo tengo ganas de preparar una sopa. Y luego comemos una ensalada de frutas.

Miguel: ¿Una ensalada de frutas? ¡No! No me gusta la fruta.

Sara: Pero te gusta la sopa, ¿no? Las sopas son nutritivas y las que yo preparo son muy ricas.

Miguel: Bueno, bueno. Comemos una sopa y luego unos sándwiches de jamón y queso, con papas fritas.

Sara: Un sándwich está bien, pero no me gustan las papas fritas. Y no son buenas para ti.

Miguel: No, Sara, no son buenas para ti, pero son muy buenas para mí. ¡Y me gustan muchísimo! Y para beber... unos refrescos.

Sara: ¿Refrescos? Pero Miguel, es importante beber agua.

Miguel: Bueno, un poco de agua en el almuerzo, pero después un helado de chocolate, unas galletas...

Sara: ¡Ay, Miguel!

Audio Scripts

LESSON 1 TEST: ESCUCHAR, ACTIVIDAD B

HL Assessment Book p. 89
HL CD 3, Track 16

La Señora Chávez piensa en lo que necesita comprar para hacer tres comidas del día. Escucha lo que ella piensa mientras está en el supermercado. Luego, lee las siguientes oraciones y decide si son ciertas o falsas. Encierra **C** o **F** en la hoja de respuestas. Corrige las oraciones falsas.

A ver... ¿qué necesito? Para el desayuno, Juan y yo comemos huevos y jamón, y bebemos jugo de naranja y café. Los chicos comen cereal con leche y beben jugo de naranja. Todos comemos pan tostado. Tengo huevos, cereal, leche y café en casa, pero necesito jamón, pan y jugo de naranja. Para el almuerzo, tengo ganas de preparar una buena sopa y unos sándwiches de jamón con queso. Luego, tomamos fruta: manzanas y uvas. A todos nos gusta mucho la fruta. Necesito comprar queso y uvas, porque tenemos manzanas. ¿Y para la cena qué necesito? ¿Una pizza? ¡Sí! Para la cena compro una pizza. Comemos la pizza con una ensalada, y después un poco de helado. Ahora compro el helado.

Audio Scripts

PRESENTACIÓN DE VOCABULARIO

Level 1 Textbook pp. 164-165

Level 1A Textbook pp. 184-186

TXT CD 3, Track 12

A. Soy Rodrigo. Vivo en Puerto Rico con mis padres. Ellos tienen dos hijos. Yo soy su hijo y mi hermana Ana es su hija. Te presento a las otras personas en nuestra familia.

B. ¿Cuántos años tienes tú? Yo tengo quince años. Ana, mi hermana menor, tiene nueve años. Soy su hermano mayor.

C. ¿Cuál es la fecha? Hoy es el primero de abril. Es mi cumpleaños. ¿Cuándo es tu cumpleaños?

¡A RESPONDER!

Level 1 Textbook p. 165

Level 1A Textbook p. 186

TXT CD 3, Track 13

Listen to the sentences about Rodrigo's family. If the sentence is true, raise your left hand. If it is false, raise your right hand.

1. María y Cristóbal son los padres de Rodrigo.
2. Camila es la tía de Ana.
3. Rodrigo es el hermano de Ana.
4. Pablo es el hermano de Ester.
5. Camila y Pablo son los padres de Tito.
6. Ana y Ester son hermanas.
7. Tito es el hijo de María.
8. José es el padre de Ana.

TELEHISTORIA - ESCENA 1

Level 1 Textbook p. 167

Level 1A Textbook p. 188

TXT CD 3, Track 14

Marisol: Señora Vélez, ¿es su cumpleaños?

Sra. Vélez: No, es el cumpleaños de Ana.

Marisol: ¡Feliz cumpleaños! ¿Cuántos años tienes?

Ana: Hoy tengo nueve años. Mañana, ¡diez!

Marisol: ¿Mañana? ¿El veintiocho de febrero?

Rodrigo: No. El primero de marzo.

Marisol: El cumpleaños de mi abuela es el primero de marzo.

Ana: Ah, ¿sí? ¿Cuántos años tiene?

Marisol: Tiene sesenta y ocho años.

Rodrigo: Mamá, ¿dónde está la camiseta? Trini Salgado está en la escuela a las cuatro.

TELEHISTORIA - ESCENA 2

Level 1 Textbook p. 172

Level 1A Textbook p. 194

TXT CD 3, Track 15

Rodrigo: ¿Dónde está la camiseta?

Sra. Vélez: ¡Ah, tus primos!

Rodrigo: Ellos comen con nosotros todos los viernes. A nuestros primos les gusta jugar al fútbol.

Sra. Vélez: ¿Camila? Es Celia. Tengo una pregunta...

Rodrigo: Es mi tía Camila. La tía Camila es la madre de Ester y Tito. Mis primos tienen catorce y diez años.

Marisol: ¿Es tu familia?

Rodrigo: Mi madre tiene dos hermanas: Inés y Mónica. Mi padre tiene un hermano, Sergio, y una hermana, Camila.

Sra. Vélez: Rodrigo, tu primo Tito tiene la camiseta de tu amiga Alicia.

Rodrigo: Mi primo tiene perros muy grandes. ¡No me gustan los perros de Tito!

PRONUNCIACIÓN

Level 1 Textbook p. 175

Level 1A Textbook p. 191

TXT CD 3, Track 16

La letra **j**

The **j** in Spanish sounds similar to the English *h* in the word *hello*.

Listen and repeat.

jamón

mujer

dibujar

joven

junio

hija

La mujer pelirroja es joven. El cumpleaños del hijo es en julio.

ACTIVIDAD 14 (17) CAPITÁN Y PRÍNCIPE

Level 1 Textbook p. 176

Level 1A Textbook, Act. 17 p. 198

TXT CD 3, Track 17

Ana is talking about her pets, Capitán and Príncipe. Listen to her description and indicate whether the following sentences are true or false.

Ana: Mi familia y yo tenemos un perro y un gato. Nuestro perro se llama Capitán y nuestro gato se llama Príncipe. Capitán es tan simpático como Príncipe, pero también son diferentes. Príncipe es mucho más pequeño que Capitán. A Príncipe le gusta descansar tanto como comer. Capitán tiene tres años; Príncipe tiene ocho años. Capitán no hace mucho; es más perezoso que Príncipe.

TELEHISTORIA COMPLETA

Level 1 Textbook p. 177

Level 1A Textbook p. 200

TXT CD 3, Track 18

Escena 1 Resumen

Mañana es el cumpleaños de Ana, la hermana de Rodrigo. Rodrigo está nervioso porque no tiene la camiseta de Alicia.

Escena 2 Resumen

Tito, el primo de Rodrigo, tiene la camiseta. A Rodrigo no le gustan los perros de Tito.

Escena 3

Marisol: ¿No te gustan los perros? Son simpáticos.

Rodrigo: Me gustan más los gatos. Son más simpáticos que los perros.

Marisol: Los perros son menos perezosos que los gatos.

Audio Scripts

Rodrigo: Los perros de Tito son perezosos y muy grandes. ¡Son tan grandes como tú!

Tito: ¡Hola, Rodrigo! Tu camiseta.

ACTIVIDAD 19(22) – INTEGRACIÓN
Level 1 Textbook p. 179
Level 1A Textbook, Act. 22 p. 202
TXT CD 3, Track 19

Read the flyer from a family looking for a new home for their dog. Then listen to the radio ad by an animal shelter. Match each dog to someone in your family and explain your choices.

FUENTE 2 ANUNCIO DE RADIO
TXT CD 3, Track 20

Listen and take notes.

¿Cómo es Dino?

¿Qué le gusta hacer a Dino?

Announcer: Sandra Calderón trabaja con la Organización para la protección de animales.

Hoy presentamos un perro muy especial. Dino es un bóxer blanco. Él tiene cinco años y es muy bonito. Siempre está tranquilo. Le gusta más descansar que correr. Es un poco perezoso pero muy divertido. La actividad favorita de Dino es mirar la televisión. Es pequeño, inteligente y muy simpático. Si usted vive en San Juan, nuestro número de teléfono es 555-6346.

LECTURA CULTURAL: LA QUINCEAÑERA
Level 1 Textbook pp. 180-181
Level 1A Textbook pp. 204-205
TXT CD 3, Track 21

La fiesta de quinceañera es muy popular en muchos países de Latinoamérica. Es similar al *Sweet Sixteen* de Estados Unidos. Muchas veces hay una ceremonia religiosa y una fiesta con banquete. En la fiesta hacen un brindis en honor a la quinceañera y después todos bailan un vals.

La chica que celebra su cumpleaños también se llama la quinceañera. En Perú (y otros países) la quinceañera tiene catorce o quince damas de honor: una por cada año que tiene. No hay un menú especial de banquete, pero en Perú es común comer comida típica del país, bailar y escuchar música tradicional.

En Puerto Rico, la celebración se llama el quinceañero. Muchas veces las chicas tienen la gran fiesta en su cumpleaños número dieciséis (por influencia del *Sweet Sixteen*) y no en el cumpleaños de los quince años.

En el banquete de una quinceañera de Puerto Rico es normal comer comida típica del país, como arroz con pollo. Todos bailan y escuchan música del Caribe: salsa, merengue, reggaetón y el hip-hop cubano.

REPASO: ACTIVIDAD 1 – LISTEN AND UNDERSTAND
Level 1 Textbook p. 184
Level 1A Textbook p. 208
TXT CD, Track 22

Marcos has a family photo and is explaining who everyone is. Listen to Marcos and then indicate each person's relationship to him.

Marcos: Hola, me llamo Marcos. Tengo una foto de toda mi familia. Mi hermano se llama Pedro y mis hermanas se llaman Elena y Rosa. Detrás de nosotros, están nuestros padres. Nuestro padre se llama Julio y nuestra madre se llama Norma. Mi abuelo se llama Alberto. Al lado de mi abuelo están mis primos. Ellos se llaman Diego y Felipe. Detrás de mis primos está mi tía. Ella se llama Carmen. Mi familia es bonita, ¿no?

Narradora: Modelo: Pedro

Pedro es el hermano de Marcos.

COMPARACIÓN CULTURAL: ¿QUÉ COMEMOS?
Level 1 Textbook pp. 186-187
Level 1A Textbook pp. 210-211
TXT CD 3, Track 23

Narrador: El Salvador. María Luisa.

María Luisa: Hola, soy María Luisa. Yo soy de El Salvador. Los domingos, voy con mi hermana mayor y mi prima a Metrocentro. Después de pasear unas horas, vamos a un café porque estamos cansadas y tenemos sed y hambre. En el café venden sándwiches, refrescos y jugos de papaya, mango, melón y otras frutas. A mí me gusta más la horchata. Es una bebida muy rica.

Narrador: Perú. Silvia.

Silvia: Yo soy Silvia y vivo en Lima, Perú. Todos los domingos comemos la cena con mis tíos. Mi tío Ricardo siempre prepara su comida favorita, el ceviche. A mí me gusta más el ají de gallina que hace mi abuela. ¡Es mejor que el ceviche de mi tío! Después de la cena, mis padres y mis tíos beben café y hablan. Mis primos y yo comemos helado y escuchamos música.

Narrador: Puerto Rico. José.

José: ¿Qué tal? Me llamo José. Vivo en San Juan, Puerto Rico. Todos los domingos, mi familia y yo comemos el almuerzo en un restaurante. Nos gusta comer carne asada. Es muy, muy buena. También me gustan los tostones. ¡Pero los tostones de mi madre son más ricos que los tostones en un restaurante!

REPASO INCLUSIVO: ACTIVIDAD 1 - LISTEN, UNDERSTAND, AND COMPARE
Level 1 Textbook pp. 188-189
Level 1A Textbook pp. 212-213
TXT CD 3, Track 24

Listen to this episode from a call-in radio show giving advice to teens. Then answer the questions.

Esperanza: Hola, Diana, ¿qué problema tienes?

Diana: Bueno, yo soy más estudiosa que mi hermano. A él y a sus amigos les gusta tocar la guitarra toda la tarde. A mí me gusta escuchar música tanto como estudiar, pero yo tengo que estudiar mucho. Tengo muchos exámenes en la clase de ciencias.

Audio Scripts

Esperanza: Hmmm... ¿Óscar es mayor o menor que tú?

Diana: Es menor que yo. Yo tengo catorce años y él tiene diez.

Esperanza: ¡Ah! Diana, tienes que aprender a vivir con tu hermano.

Diana: Pero, ¿qué necesito hacer?

Esperanza: Necesitas hablar con Óscar. Tú estudias de las tres a las cinco de la tarde. Tu hermano y sus amigos tocan la guitarra de las cinco a las siete, y tú escuchas.

Diana: Está bien. ¡Gracias!

WORKBOOK SCRIPTS
WB CD 2

INTEGRACIÓN HABLAR

Level 1 Workbook p. 131

Level 1A Workbook p. 133

WB CD 2, Track 11

Listen to the principal's loudspeaker message on the first day of the school year. Take notes.

FUENTE 2

WB CD 2, Track 12

¡Hola a todos! ¡Ya no es un secreto! Nuestra maestra de español es familia del presidente. ¡Les presento a la maestra! Ella es muy simpática, inteligente y tiene treinta años. Ella es la hija de un hermano del presidente. Sí, el presidente es su tío, porque es hermano de su padre. Ella siempre habla por teléfono con el presidente y con la hija del presidente, que se llama María Graciela.

INTEGRACIÓN ESCRIBIR

Level 1 Workbook p. 132

Level 1A Workbook p. 134

WB CD 2, Track 13

Listen to the radio talk show about señor Juan. Take notes.

FUENTE 2

WB CD 2, Track 14

¡Hola! Hoy hablamos del Sr. Juan Márquez. Es el hombre más viejo del país. Hoy, él está todo el día con su familia. Tiene una familia de ciento cuarenta y dos personas. Su fecha de nacimiento es el 23 de enero de mil novecientos dos. Es mayor que todas las personas del país. ¡Feliz cumpleaños, señor Márquez!

ESCUCHAR A, ACTIVIDAD 1

Level 1 Workbook p. 133

Level 1A Workbook p. 135

WB CD 2, Track 15

Listen to Enrique and take notes. Then, match the names with the family relationship that each person has to Enrique.

Enrique: Hola, me llamo Enrique. Tengo una hermana. Ella se llama Sofía. Mis padres se llaman Alicia y Jorge. Mi madre tiene una hermana mayor que se llama Norma. Norma tiene dos hijos. Ellos se llaman Raúl y Julia. Mis abuelos se llaman Ernesto y Luisa.

ESCUCHAR A, ACTIVIDAD 2

Level 1 Workbook p. 133

Level 1A Workbook p. 135

WB CD 2, Track 16

Listen to Sofía and take notes. Then, complete the sentences below.

Sofía: Hola, soy Sofía. Mi hermano mayor se llama Enrique. En diciembre mis padres, mi hermano y yo vamos a Puerto Rico. Mis abuelos viven en San Juan. Tengo mucha familia en Puerto Rico. Mis tíos y mis primos viven cerca de mis abuelos. Me gusta estar con mis primos más que con mis amigos. José, mi primo mayor, es muy inteligente.

ESCUCHAR B, ACTIVIDAD 1

Level 1 Workbook p. 134

Level 1A Workbook p. 136

WB CD 2, Track 17

Listen to Jimena and take notes. Then, indicate which family members Jimena has and doesn't have by putting the following words in the correct column.

Jimena: Hola, me llamo Jimena. Mi familia no es muy grande. Mi padre se llama Manuel. No tengo madre pero mi madrastra es muy simpática. Ella se llama Lorena. Sabrina es mi hermana. Nosotras no tenemos hermanos. Tengo dos abuelas pero no tengo abuelos. Mis abuelas viven en Ponce. Tengo cuatro primas. No tengo primos. Ellas son las hijas de mi tía Paula. Hay más chicas que chicos en mi familia.

ESCUCHAR B, ACTIVIDAD 2

Level 1 Workbook p. 134

Level 1A Workbook p. 136

WB CD 2, Track 18

Listen to Enrique and take notes. Then, answer the following questions.

Enrique: Todos los viernes, mi prima Blanca y yo comemos con nuestros abuelos. Blanca es más divertida que todos mis amigos. Ella lee mucho, toca la guitarra y prepara la comida. Nosotros siempre preparamos la comida con nuestros abuelos. La comida de mi abuela es tan buena como la comida de mi padre. Después de comer, miramos la televisión o paseamos con los abuelos.

ESCUCHAR C, ACTIVIDAD 1

Level 1 Workbook p. 135

Level 1A Workbook p. 137

WB CD 2, Track 19

Listen to Mariano and take notes. Then explain how the following people are related to him by filling in the blank with the appropriate word.

Mariano: Me llamo Mariano. Vivo en Ponce con mi familia. Tengo una familia grande. Mis abuelos se llaman Ramón y Teresa. Son los padres de mi madre. Mi madre es Carmen y mi padre se llama Felipe. Tengo dos hermanos y una hermana. Mis hermanos son mayores. Se llaman Luis y Tomás. Mi hermana es menor. Ella se llama Anita. Mis primos viven en Ponce también. Mi primo Javier y yo somos mejores amigos. Él es el hijo de mis tíos Marcos y Diana.

Audio Scripts

ESCUCHAR C, ACTIVIDAD 2

Level 1 Workbook p. 135
Level 1A Workbook p. 137
WB CD 2, Track 20

Listen to Lucía and take notes. Then answer the questions below in complete sentences.

Lucía: Hola, soy Lucía. Me gusta mucho pasear un rato con mis primos. Ellos son más divertidos que mi hermana. Mis primos son mayores que yo pero son más jóvenes que mi hermana. A mis primos les gusta andar en patineta tanto como montar en bicicleta. Mi hermana es simpática, pero es más seria que yo. Le gusta más estudiar que jugar.

ASSESSMENT SCRIPTS
TEST CD 1

LESSON 2 TEST:
ESCUCHAR ACTIVIDAD A

Modified Assessment Book p. 95
On-level Assessment Book p. 125
Pre-AP Assessment Book p. 95

TEST CD 1, Track 17

Narrador: Listen to the following audio. Then complete Activity A.

Juan: Mi familia es muy grande. Mis padres se llaman Ricardo y Linda. Mi madre es más atlética que mi padre pero mi padre es más artístico. Tengo dos hermanos menores. Andrés tiene cinco años y Daniel tiene diez años. A ellos les gusta practicar deportes. Mis abuelos son de Puerto Rico. Tienen setenta y cinco años. Mi tía Elena tiene treinta y cinco años. Ella es la hermana menor de mi madre. Mi tía Elena tiene dos hijos, Iván y Sandra. Ellos son mis primos. Son muy simpáticos y me gusta mucho pasar el rato con ellos. Mañana, 4 de octubre, es el cumpleaños de mi madre. ¡Feliz cumpleaños, mamá!

LESSON 2 TEST:
ESCUCHAR ACTIVIDAD B

Modified Assessment Book p. 95
On-level Assessment Book p. 125
Pre-AP Assessment Book p. 95

TEST CD 1, Track 18

Narrador: Listen to the following audio. Then complete Activity B.

Clara: El 10 de enero es el cumpleaños del abuelo Antonio.

Mamá: Sí, y el 1 de febrero es el cumpleaños de tu abuela Ana.

Clara: Sí, mamá. ¡La abuela Ana tiene setenta y cinco años este año! El 25 de marzo es el cumpleaños de mi padre.

Mamá: Sí, Clara. Él tiene cincuenta años.

Clara: El 8 de agosto es el cumpleaños de la tía Cecilia.

Mamá: Tía Cecilia es muy joven. Es mi hermana menor. El 18 de octubre es un cumpleaños muy importante, ¿no?

Clara: ¡Sí, mamá, es mi cumpleaños!

UNIT 3 TEST:
ESCUCHAR ACTIVIDAD A

Modified Assessment Book p. 107
On-level Assessment Book p. 137
Pre-AP Assessment Book p. 107

TEST CD 1, Track 19

Narrador: Listen to the following audio. Then complete Activity A.

1. Mariana es la madre de mi madre.
2. Carlos y Pedro son los hijos de mi tía.
3. Julia es la hermana de mi padre.
4. Samuel es el hijo de mi padre y mi madre.
5. Javier es el padre de mi padre.

UNIT 3 TEST:
ESCUCHAR ACTIVIDAD B

Modified Assessment Book p. 107
On-level Assessment Book p. 137
Pre-AP Assessment Book p. 107

TEST CD 1, Track 20

Narrador: Listen to the following audio. Then complete Activity B.

Felipe: ¿A qué hora desayunas?

Marta: Desayuno a las siete de la mañana.

Felipe: ¿Qué te gusta comer para el desayuno?

Marta: Me gusta el cereal con leche y una banana. Siempre bebo un vaso de jugo de naranja. Es un desayuno muy nutritivo, ¿no?

Felipe: ¿No comes huevos en la mañana?

Marta: No me gustan los huevos.

Felipe: ¿Qué te gusta comer para el almuerzo?

Marta: Siempre como en la cafetería de la escuela. Todos los días tienen comida diferente. Muchas veces como una hamburguesa o un sándwich.

Felipe: ¿Tienes hambre después de la escuela?

Marta: Sí. A veces como un yogur o una fruta, pero si tengo mucha hambre comparto una pizza con mis amigos.

HERITAGE LEARNERS SCRIPTS
HL CDS 1 & 3

INTEGRACIÓN HABLAR

Level 1 HL Workbook p. 133
Level 1A HL Workbook p. 112
HL CD 1, Track 21

Escucha a Lucía hablando de las fotos de su reunión familiar.

FUENTE 2

HL CD 1, Track 22

Estas son las fotos de nuestra reunión familiar. Aquí están todos nuestros tíos y también los primos y mi sobrinita. Vinieron desde muy lejos para estar presentes. Todos mis hermanos hablan dos idiomas. Nos gusta mucho el inglés y también nos gusta el español. Pero mis primos no hablan inglés. Mi prima tiene solamente diez años pero mi primo es mayor. Él tiene dieciséis. En esta foto estamos comiendo. A mí me gustan las hamburguesas y los sándwiches pero a mis primos no les gusta eso. Ellos solamente comen sopa, arroz y carne. ¡Pero me gustan mucho mis primos!

INTEGRACIÓN ESCRIBIR

Level 1 Workbook p. 134
Level 1A Workbook p. 113

Audio Scripts

HL CD 1, Track 23

Escucha el siguiente anuncio de radio. Toma apuntes.

FUENTE 2

HL CD 1, Track 24

¡Conoce a nuestra Asociación de Hispanoamericanos! Somos un grupo de unas 500 personas que vivimos en Texas pero que somos de origen latinoamericano. Nuestra asociación va a celebrar una Feria Puertorriqueña este año en el Hotel Lago Azul. Será una gran fiesta familiar, con padres, madres, abuelos, tíos y primos. ¡Hasta los perros y los gatos pueden venir! Como todos los años, tendremos la competencia de comida tradicional. La fecha será el 3 de abril. Esperamos ver más de mil personas allí.

LESSON 2 TEST: ESCUCHAR, ACTIVIDAD A

HL Assessment Book p. 101

HL CD 3, Track 17

Escucha mientras Teresa describe a su familia. Luego contesta las preguntas con oraciones completas.

Teresa: ¡Hola! Soy Teresa Aguilar y vivo con mi familia. Somos tres hermanos: Juan es el mayor y tiene veinte años. Es un chico muy inteligente. Mi hermana Anita es la más pequeña de la familia; tiene tan sólo diez años. A Anita le gustan los perros y los gatos. Tenemos un perro muy grande y dos gatos en casa. Yo tengo quince años y me gusta muchísimo la música. Mis padres son muy organizados y enseñan en la universidad. Mi abuela vive con nosotros también. Ella tiene casi setenta años. Es simpatiquísima. También tengo primos. Paso mucho tiempo con ellos porque viven cerca de nuestra casa. Mañana, primero de abril, es el cumpleaños de una de mis tías. ¡Habrá una fiesta fantástica en su casa!

LESSON 2 TEST: ESCUCHAR, ACTIVIDAD B

HL Assessment Book p. 101

HL CD 3, Track 18

Ángela es una niña a quien le gusta hacer muchas preguntas. Escucha la conversación que tiene con su abuela y luego contesta las preguntas con oraciones completas.

Ángela: Abuelita, ¿quién es mayor, tú o abuelito?

Abuela: El abuelito es mayor, Ángela. Abuelo tiene casi ochenta años y yo sólo tengo setenta.

Ángela: ¿Tienes setenta años? Entonces, ¿eres mayor o menor que el tío Carlos?

Abuela: Bueno, tu tío Carlos cumple cincuenta años en junio. Soy mayor que él. Y él es menor que yo.

Ángela: ¿Y eres mayor que mi otra abuela, la abuelita Lola?

Abuela: Bueno, soy tan joven como ella. Las dos tenemos setenta años.

Ángela: Y mi prima Sandra... ¿es más joven que mi primo Alex?

Abuela: No. No es menor que Alex. Los dos tienen quince años.

Ángela: Y, por fin, abuelita, ¿quién de la familia es tan joven como yo?

Abuela: Nadie, Angelita. Eres la más jovencita de la familia.

UNIT 3 TEST: ESCUCHAR, ACTIVIDAD A

HL Assessment Book p. 113

HL CD 3, Track 19

Pablo y Antonio hablan de lo que les gusta comer y beber. Escucha su conversación y lee las siguientes oraciones. Decide si las oraciones son ciertas o falsas y encierra en un círculo **C** o **F** en la hoja de respuestas.

Antonio: Buenos días, Pablo. ¿Qué desayunas hoy?

Pablo: Lo de siempre, Antonio: cereal con leche, un huevo, pan tostado y un jugo de naranja. ¿Y tú?

Antonio: Yo solamente bebo un café y como dos o tres galletas. Me gustan las galletas.

Pablo: Pero tu desayuno no es nutritivo.

Antonio: Bueno, a las once de la mañana siempre compro algo, por ejemplo un helado o un refresco.

Pablo: Eso no está bien. Debes comer yogur o un poco de fruta.

Antonio: ¿Yogur? ¡Puaj! El yogur es horrible. No me gusta.

Pablo: No, Antonio, el yogur es rico y nutritivo. ¿Y qué comes tú al almuerzo?

Antonio: Al almuerzo como bien: una hamburguesa con queso, unas papas fritas, y dos o tres refrescos.

Pablo: Mira, esta tarde vamos a comprar fruta. En la Frutería Manolo venden muchas frutas deliciosas.

Antonio: Está bien. Comeré fruta hoy.

UNIT 3 TEST: ESCUCHAR, ACTIVIDAD B

HL Assessment Book p. 113

HL CD 3, Track 20

Escucha lo que dice Sara de un día especial de su familia. Luego contesta las preguntas con oraciones completas.

Sara: Hola, soy Sara. Hoy es el primero de mayo. Es un día especial porque es el cumpleaños de mi abuelo. Él cumple ochenta años y es cinco años mayor que mi abuela. Los abuelos viven cerca de nuestra casa, con mis tíos Ricardo y Sofía. Mis tíos tienen una hija que es menor que yo y un hijo que es mayor que yo. Se llaman Patricia y Raúl y tienen trece y diecisiete años. Mamá tiene otra hermana, Julia, que pasará unos días en nuestra casa para el cumpleaños del abuelo. Tía Julia no tiene hijos, pero tiene un perro muy simpático. ¡Ah! Y todos los hermanos de mi padre también están aquí para celebrar ese día especial. La familia de papá es muy grande: son cuatro hermanos y tres hermanas y todos tienen muchos hijos. Yo no tengo hermanos pero tengo muchísimos primos y primas. ¡Feliz cumpleaños, abuelito!

Map/Culture Activities *Puerto Rico*

1 Puerto Rico is a small island in a group of islands called the Greater Antilles
(**Antillas Mayores**). Which other islands are part of this group? Label them on the
map below. On which of these islands is Spanish the primary language spoken?
Circle them on the map.

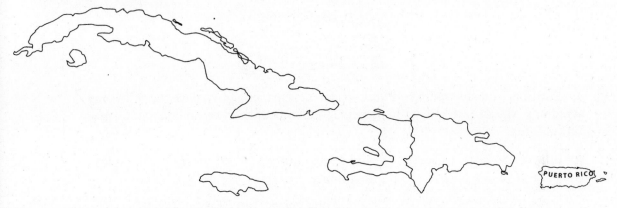

2 Which body of water lies between the United States and the north of Puerto Rico?
Label it on the map. Which body of water can be found between South America and
the south of Puerto Rico? Label it on the map.

Map/Culture Activities *Puerto Rico*

3 Imagine that you are reading a Puerto Rican newspaper and you see the following headlines. Match each one with the person that most likely would be mentioned in each article.

1. Julia de Burgos

2. Roberto Clemente

3. Rosario Ferré

4. Luís Muñoz Marín

a. _____ publica un libro nuevo con versiones en inglés y español.

b. _____ escribe una nueva colección de poemas.

c. _____ gana (*wins*) la Serie Mundial de béisbol con los Pittsburgh Pirates.

d. _____ gana (*wins*) las elecciones del Senado (*Senate*) de Puerto Rico.

4 In Puerto Rico, many families enjoy tamales wrapped in banana leaves (**pasteles**) and yellow rice with peas (**arroz con gandules**) at Christmastime. What are some traditional foods that your family prepares for specific holidays? Which country or culture do those dishes come from?

_____

_____

_____

_____

5 Do the colorful houses that are typical of San Juan's colonial quarter, known as **Viejo San Juan**, resemble houses where you live? How are they similar or different?

_____

_____

_____

_____

UNIDAD 3

Map/Culture Activities

Map/Culture Activities Answer Key

PUERTO RICO

Page 83

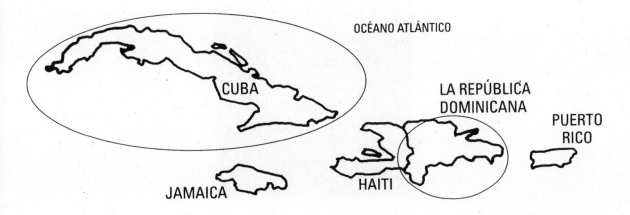

OCÉANO ATLÁNTICO

CUBA

LA REPÚBLICA
DOMINICANA

PUERTO
RICO

JAMAICA

HAITI

MAR CARIBE

❶ Refer to map above.

❷ Refer to map above.

Page 84

❸ **1.** b   **2.** c   **3.** a   **4.** d

❹ Answers will vary.

❺ Answers will vary.

Fine Art Activities

La Plaza de Colón, Manuel Hernández Acevedo

Perhaps best known for his serigraphs, or fine art silk screens, Puerto Rican artist Manuel Hernández Acevedo started out as an apprentice sign painter and cook. Despite his lack of formal artistic training, his paintings remain popular for their simplicity and expressive use of color and light. The city of Old San Juan in Puerto Rico was his favorite subject, and most of his paintings, like *La Plaza de Colón*, focus on street scenes, plazas and neighborhoods in the area.

1. **a.** Do you think the perspective in *La Plaza de Colón* is realistic? Why or why not?

_____

_____

_____

b. Explain the reasons the artist may have had for choosing this perspective in the painting.

_____

_____

_____

2. How does the painting give you a sense of the city around it? Use details to describe what you think the city of Old San Juan might be like, based on your observations from *La Plaza de Colón*.

_____

_____

_____

_____

_____

La Plaza de Colón (1986), Manuel Hernández Acevedo. Oil on board. Collection of Arte de la Cooperativa de Seguros Múltiples, San Juan, Puerto Rico. © 2005 Víctor Manuel Hernández/Estate of Manuel Hernández Acevedo.

Fine Art Activities

Cantor criollo, **Augusto Marín**

Puerto Rican artist Augusto Marín is skilled in a variety of artistic media including drawing, stained glass, and lithograph. He is well known for the many public and private murals on display throughout Puerto Rico and for his attention to color, light, and shadow. The geometric style of *Cantor criollo* shows the influence of Spanish artist Pablo Picasso, while the detail, tone, and palette of the painting are uniquely Marín.

Complete the following activities based on your study of *Cantor criollo*, by Augusto Marín.

1. The figure seated on the floor is playing a traditional Caribbean instrument called a *cuatro*. Look at the man and use examples to explain how the artist has used line and shape to draw attention to the delicate action he performs.

   _____

   _____

   _____

   _____

   _____

   _____

2. How does Marín create a sense of serenity in the painting? Describe the specific images, colors and techniques that contribute to the calm mood of *Cantor criollo*.

   _____

   _____

   _____

   _____

Cantor criollo (1962), Augusto Marín. Oil on masonite, 48"x 44". Collection of Arte de la Cooperativa Seguros Múltiples, San Juan, Puerto Rico. Courtesy of Lisi Marín, San Juan, Puerto Rico.

Fine Art Activities

Goyita, Rafael Tufiño

Rafael Tufiño was born in New York to Puerto Rican parents. At the age of ten he relocated to Puerto Rico, where he developed an interest in a range of artistic activities including painting and drawing. Tufiño honed his talents during years of study and travel throughout Latin America, eventually gaining recognition for his paintings, drawings, prints and fine art posters. Tufiño has worked actively to promote the cultural identity and art of Puerto Rico, and uses his work to explore social issues including poverty, race relations, and gender roles.

Study Rafael Tufiño's painting, *Goyita*, and complete the following activities.

1. Identify what you think the artist's attitude is toward the subject of *Goyita*, and explain how Tufiño incorporated emotion into the work.

   _____

   _____

   _____

   _____

2. How do the images presented in *Goyita* compare with your ideas about who and what make up the nation of Puerto Rico? Compare and contrast your knowledge and opinions of Puerto Rico with those presented in the painting.

   _____

   _____

   _____

   _____

   _____

   _____

Goyita (1949), Rafael Tufiño. Oil on canvas, 25 1/2" x 21". Photograph by John Betancourt. Courtesy of Pablo Tufiño.

Fine Art Activities

José Campeche at the Door to Old San Juan, Lorenzo Homar

José Campeche at the Door to Old San Juan (1976), Lorenzo Homar. Screen print. Graphic Arts Collection. Department of Rare Books and Special Collections. Princeton University/ Courtesy of the Homar Family.

At the age of fifteen, Lorenzo Homar moved from Puerto Rico to the United States. After completing his education in New York, Homar worked as a jewelry designer for Cartier, and later fought in the South Pacific during World War II as a member of the U.S. Army. Homar returned to his homeland in 1950, dedicating himself to graphic art. He is considered Puerto Rico's finest graphic artist and has received international acclaim for his caricatures, silkscreen prints, woodcuts, and paintings.

Complete the following activities based on your observations of *Jose Campeche at the Door to Old San Juan*, a silkscreen by Lorenzo Homar.

1. José Campeche brought Puerto Rican art to an international level during the eighteenth century and is considered the father of Puerto Rican painting. How do you think Homar feels about Campeche? Describe the artist's attitude toward his subject as presented in *José Campeche at the Door*.

    _____
    _____
    _____
    _____
    _____

2. What might the position of Campeche at the doors of Old San Juan symbolize? Explain the symbolism inherent in the artist's choice of background.

    _____
    _____
    _____
    _____
    _____

Fine Art Activities Answer Key

LA PLAZA COLÓN, MANUEL HERNÁNDEZ ACEVEDO
p. 86

1a. Answers will vary. Students should be able to recognize the unusual perspective of the painting, which makes it appear almost dimensionless.

b. Answers will vary. Students may cite lack of formal training, or the possibility of broadening the scope of the painting.

2. Answers will vary. Students should give specific examples from the work in their response.

CANTOR CRIOLLO, AUGUSTO MARÍN
p. 87

1. Answers will vary. Students should focus on the way in which the lines and geometric shapes composing the figure direct the viewer's eye to the movement of his fingers over the more organic–looking cuatro.

2. Answers will vary. Students may focus on one or all of the painting's features. The figure is in a relaxed posture with eyes closed. The colors are neutral and in agreement; the form of the painting draws the viewer to the center of the work.

GOYITA, RAFAEL TUFIÑO
p. 88

1. Answers will vary. This painting is a tribute to Tufiño's mother, who represented for the artist the face of Puerto Rico's ethnic and social reality. This is an honest, unadorned rendering of the subject. Though somewhat harsh, the uplifted head and resolute eyes of the subject clearly imply the respect Tufiño felt for the working women of Puerto Rico.

2. Answers will vary. Students should be specific in their answers.

JOSÉ CAMPECHE AT THE DOOR TO OLD SAN JUAN, LORENZO HOMAR
p. 89

1. Answers will vary. This silkscreen pays homage to Campeche and depicts the artist in a strong, intense, and dignified manner.

2. Answers will vary. Campeche himself represents a door or window into the life and landscape of Old San Juan, a thriving city and the capital of Puerto Rico during Campeche's time.

Date: _____

Dear Family:

    We are about to begin Unidad 3, of the Level 1 ¡Avancemos! program. It focuses on authentic culture and real-life communication using Spanish in Puerto Rico. It practices reading, writing, listening, and speaking, and introduces students to culture typical of Puerto Rico.

    Through completing the activities, students will employ critical thinking skills as they compare the Spanish language and the culture of Puerto Rico with their own community. They will also connect to other academic subjects, using their knowledge of Spanish to access new information. In this unit, students are learning to discuss foods and beverages, dates, months, family members, numbers from 200 to 1,000,000, and questions words. They are also learning about grammar—the verb tener (to have), the verb hacer (to make or to do), forming questions with interrogative words, and present tense -er and -ir verbs.

    Please feel free to call me with any questions or concerns you might have as your student practices reading, writing, listening, and speaking in Spanish.

Sincerely,

Nombre _____ Clase _____ Fecha _____

Family Involvement Activity

STEP 1
Distribute several copies of this chart to each player. The goal of the game is to take turns filling each category with as many names as you can think of in a limited time.

Country (País)	Food (Comida)	Family Member (Miembro de la familia)	Pets (Mascotas)	Clothing (Ropa)	Score
T	O	T	A	L	

STEP 2
One team member is selected to silently say the letters of the alphabet. After several seconds, the player to the right says, **"¡BASTA!"** The first player stops reciting the alphabet and tells the rest of the group the letter he or she had in mind.

STEP 3
Players must then try to fill in the chart with as many words for each category as they can. All the words must start with the selected alphabet letter. The first to finish shouts, **"¡BASTA!"** At this point, all other players must stop writing.

STEP 4
The player who finishes first reads the words from each category. The other players compare their answers with those of the first player, and use the score criteria listed below to add up their points.

STEP 5
Continue to the second category and so on until you have scored all the categories. Add up all points and write them down on the scoring table. Play at least ten times. When the players read the words, try translating them into Spanish and keep a record of the words you can translate. At the end of the game, write down the total number of words you can translate. Also write the final score for each of the family members who participated in the game.

Score Criteria:
If the word you wrote down is valid (it belongs in the category and begins with the predetermined letter) but has not been written down by any other player, you score 10 points. If the word you wrote down is valid, but also appears on another player's chart, you each score 5 points.

Absent Student Copymasters

Presentación / Práctica de vocabulario

Materials Checklist

☐ Student text

☐ DVD 1

☐ Video activities copymasters

☐ TXT CD 3 tracks 1–2

☐ *Cuaderno* pages 99–101 (L1A pp. 101–103)

☐ *Cuaderno para hispanohablantes* pages 99–102 (L1A pp. 101–104)

☐ Did You Get It? Copymasters pages 1, 2, and 10

Steps to Follow

☐ Study the vocabulary of **Presentación de vocabulario** (L1 pp. 140–141, L1A pp. 156–158) by reading the words above the photos and the accompanying text. Watch the vocabulary video for **Unidad 3**, **Lección 1** and complete the video activities copymaster.

☐ Practice the words in the **Más vocabulario** box on page 140 (L1A p. 157). Read the words aloud. Write the words in your notebook.

☐ Read the vocabulary words again as you listen to their pronunciations on the CD. Repeat the words aloud.

☐ Do **Práctica de vocabulario** (L1 p. 142, L1A p. 159). Complete **Actividades 1** and **2** on page 142 (L1A p. 159).

☐ Complete *Cuaderno* pages 99, 100, and 101 (L1A pp. 101–103).
OR
Complete *Cuaderno para hispanohablantes* pages 99, 100, 101, and 102 (L1A pp. 101–103).

☐ Complete the **Para y piensa** box on page 142 (L1A p. 159).

☐ Complete the Did You Get It? Copymasters, pages 1, 2, and 10.

If You Don't Understand . . .

☐ Watch the DVD in a quiet place. If you get lost, stop and go back.

☐ Listen to the CD in a quiet place. If you get lost, stop the CD and go back.

☐ Re-read the directions for the activity you find difficult. Write out the directions in your own words.

☐ Read the model before starting so you know what to do. Follow the model.

☐ If the activity has parts for two people, practice both parts.

Absent Student Copymasters

Level 1 pp. 143–144
Level 1A pp. 160–161

Vocabulario en contexto

Materials Checklist

☐ Student text

☐ DVD 1

☐ Video activities copymasters

☐ TXT CD 3 track 3

☐ Did You Get It? Copymasters pages 1, 3, and 11

Steps to Follow

☐ Look at the photo and read the caption on page 143 (L1A p. 160).

☐ Read **Cuando lees** and **Cuando escuchas** under *Strategies* (L1 p. 143, L1A p. 160). Copy the questions.

☐ Answer the question in **Cuando lees** before watching the video.

☐ Watch the **Unidad 3, Lección 1Telehistoria escena 1** without your book. Then watch the DVD again and complete the video activities copymaster.

☐ Look at the dialogue in the book. Follow along in the book as you listen to the CD. Use the picture and context clues to help you understand the dialogue.

☐ Study the words in the **También se dice** box.

☐ Complete **Actividades 3** and **4** (L1 p. 144, L1A p. 161).

☐ Complete the **Para y piensa** box on page 144 (L1A p. 161).

☐ Complete the Did You Get It? Copymasters, pages 1, 3, and 11.

If You Don't Understand . . .

☐ Watch the DVD in a quiet place. Review sections that seemed confusing.

☐ Listen to the CD in a quiet place. If you get lost, stop the CD and go back.

☐ Re-read the directions for any activity you find difficult. Write out the directions in your own words.

☐ Read the model before starting so you know what to do. Follow the model.

☐ Read aloud everything that you write.

☐ If you have any questions, write them down so you can ask your teacher later.

Absent Student Copymasters

Presentación / Práctica de gramática

Materials Checklist

- [ ] Student text
- [ ] TXT CD 3 track 4
- [ ] *Cuaderno* pages 102–104 (L1A pp. 104–106)
- [ ] *Cuaderno para hispanohablantes* pages 103–105 (L1A pp. 105–107)
- [ ] Did You Get It? Copymasters pages 4 and 5
- [ ] ClassZone.com

Steps to Follow

- [ ] Study the verb **gustar** with the nouns on page 145 (L1A p. 12).
- [ ] Complete **Actividad 5** (L1 p. 146).
- [ ] Complete **Actividads 5** and **6** (L1A p. 163).
- [ ] Listen to TXT CD 3 track 4 as you follow along in the Pronunciación activity on p 146 (LIA p. 163).
- [ ] Complete **Actividades 7, 8**, and **9** (L1 p. 147).
- [ ] Complete **Actividades 7, 8, 9, 10**, and **11** (L1A pp. 164–165).
- [ ] Complete *Cuaderno* pages 102, 103, and 104 (L1A pp. 104–106).
  OR
  Complete *Cuaderno para hispanohablantes* pages 103, 104, and 105 (L1A pp. 105–107).
- [ ] Check your comprehension by completing the **Para y piensa** box on page 147 (L1A p. 165).
- [ ] Complete the Did You Get It? Copymasters, pages 4 and 5.

If You Don't Understand . . .

- [ ] For activities that require listening, listen to the CD in a quiet place. If you get lost, stop the CD and go back.
- [ ] Write out the directions in your own words.
- [ ] Read the model a few times so you are certain that you understand what to do.
- [ ] If you have any questions, write them down for your teacher.
- [ ] Use the Animated Grammar to help you understand.
- [ ] Use the Leveled Grammar Practice on the @Home Tutor.

Absent Student Copymasters

UNIDAD 3 Lección 1

Absent Student Copymasters

Gramática en contexto

Materials Checklist

☐ Student text

☐ DVD 1

☐ Video activities copymasters

☐ TXT CD 3, track 5

☐ Did You Get It? Copymasters pages 4 and 6

Steps to Follow

☐ Examine the photo on page 148 (L1A p. 166). What do you think is happening?

☐ Read **Cuando lees** and **Cuando escuchas** under *Strategies* (L1 p. 148, L1A p. 166).

☐ Watch the **Unidad 3, Lección 1 Telehistoria escena 2** without your book. Then watch the DVD again and complete the video activities copymasters.

☐ Look at the dialogue in the book. Follow along in the book as you listen to the CD. Use the pictures and context to help you understand the dialogue.

☐ Complete **Actividades 10, 11,** and **12** (L1 p. 149).

☐ Complete **Actividades 12, 13,** and **14** (L1A p. 167).

☐ Check your comprehension by completing the **Para y piensa** box on page 149 (L1A p. 167).

☐ Complete the Did You Get It? Copymasters, pages 4 and 6.

If You Don't Understand . . .

☐ Go to a quiet place and watch the DVD. If you get lost, stop it and play it again.

☐ Listen to the CD in a quiet place. If you get lost, stop the CD and go back.

☐ Write out the directions in your own words.

☐ Read the model a few times so you are certain that you understand what to do.

☐ Read aloud everything that you write. Be sure that you understand what you are reading.

☐ If you have any questions, write them down for your teacher to answer later.

☐ If the activity has parts for two people, do both parts of the activity.

☐ Think about what you are trying to say when you write a sentence. After you write your sentence, check to make sure that it says what you wanted to say.

Absent Student Copymasters

Presentación / Práctica de gramática

Materials Checklist

☐ Student text

☐ *Cuaderno* pages 105–107 (L1A pp. 107–109)

☐ *Cuaderno para hispanohablantes* pages 106–109 (L1A pp. 108–111)

☐ TXT CD 1 track 6

☐ Did You Get It? Copymasters pages 7 and 8

☐ ClassZone.com

Steps to Follow

☐ Study the conjugation of the present tense of **–er** and **–ir** verbs on page 150 (L1A p. 168).

☐ Complete **Actividades 13, 14, 15,** and **16** (L1 pp. 151–152).

☐ Complete **Actividades 15, 16, 17, 18, 19,** and **20** (L1A pp. 169–171).

☐ Complete *Cuaderno* pages 105, 106, and 107 (L1A pp. 107–109).
   OR
   Complete *Cuaderno para hispanohablantes* pages 106, 107, 108, and 109 (L1A pp. 108–111).

☐ Check your comprehension by completing the **Para y piensa** box on page 152 (L1A p. 171).

☐ Complete the Did You Get It? Copymasters pages 7 and 8.

If You Don't Understand . . .

☐ For activities that require listening, listen to the CD in a quiet place. If you get lost, stop the CD and go back.

☐ Re-read the directions for the activity you find difficult. Write out the directions in your own words.

☐ Write the model on your paper. Try to follow the model in your own answers.

☐ If the activity has parts for two people, practice both parts.

☐ Think about what you are trying to say when you write a sentence. After you write your sentence, check to make sure that it says what you wanted to say.

☐ Use the Animated Grammar to help you understand.

☐ Use the Leveled Grammar Practice on the @Home Tutor.

Absent Student Copymasters

UNIDAD 3 Lección 1

Absent Student Copymasters

Todo junto

Materials Checklist

- [ ] Student text
- [ ] DVD 1
- [ ] Video activities copymasters
- [ ] *Cuaderno* pages 108–109 (L1A pp. 110–111)
- [ ] *Cuaderno para hispanohablantes* pages 110–111 (L1A pp. 112–113)
- [ ] Did You Get It? Copymasters pages 7 and 9
- [ ] WB CD 2 tracks 1–4
- [ ] HL CD 1 tracks 17–20
- [ ] TXT CD 3 tracks 7–9

Steps to Follow

- [ ] Look at the photos on page 153 (L1A p. 172). Think about what is happening in the pictures.
- [ ] Read **Cuando lees** and **Cuando escuchas** under *Strategies* (L1 p. 153, L1A p. 172). Copy the questions.
- [ ] Review the content of **Unidad 3, Telehistoria escena 1** and **escena 2**.
- [ ] Watch the **Unidad 3, Telehistoria escena 3 Lección 1** without your book. Then watch the DVD again and complete the video activities copymaster.
- [ ] Complete **Actividades 17, 18**, and **19** (L1 p. 154).
- [ ] Complete **Actividades 21, 22**, and **23** (L1A p. 173).
- [ ] Do **Actividades 20** and **21** (L1 p. 155).
- [ ] Do **Actividades 24** and **25** (L1A p. 174).
- [ ] Complete *Cuaderno* pages 108 and 109 (L1A pp. 110–111).
  OR
  Complete *Cuaderno para hispanohablantes* pages 110 and 111 (L1A pp. 112–113).
- [ ] Complete the Did You Get It? Copymasters, pages 7 and 9.

If You Don't Understand . . .

- [ ] Re-read the directions for the activity you find difficult. Write out the directions in your own words.

Absent Student Copymasters

Lectura y Conexiones

Materials Checklist

☐ Student text

☐ TXT CD 3 track 10

Steps to Follow

☐ Read and complete **Strategy: Leer** (L1 p. 156, L1A p. 176).

☐ Read the ad and the shopping list. **¡A comprar y a comer!** on pages 156 and 157 (L1A pp. 176–177).

☐ Follow along with the text on TXT CD 3, track 10.

☐ Check your comprehension by completing the **¿Comprendiste?** and **¿Y tú?** sections of **Para y piensa** on page 157 (L1A p. 177).

☐ Read **Los huracanes** on page 158 (L1A p. 178).

☐ Read **Proyecto 1**, **Las matemáticas**, and try to make the calculation.

☐ Do the research as directed in **Proyecto 2**, **La historia**.

☐ Read **La geografía** in **Proyecto 3**. Make a chart with all the information requested in the exercise.

If You Don't Understand . . .

☐ Listen to the CD as many times as necessary.

☐ Read everything aloud. Be sure that you understand what you are reading.

☐ If you have any questions, write them down so you can ask your teacher later.

☐ Think about what you are trying to say when you write a sentence. After you write your sentence, check to make sure that it says what you wanted to say.

Absent Student Copymasters

Repaso de la lección

Materials Checklist

- ☐ Student text
- ☐ *Cuaderno* pages 113–121
- ☐ *Cuaderno para hispanohablantes* pages 112–121
- ☐ WB CD 2 tracks 5–10
- ☐ TXT CD 3 track 11

Steps to Follow

- ☐ Read the bullet points under ¡**Llegada!** on page 160 (L1A p. 180).
- ☐ Complete **Actividades 1, 2, 3, 4**, and **5** (L1 pp. 160–161, L1A pp. 180–181).
- ☐ Complete *Cuaderno* pages 110, 111, and 112 (L1A pp. 112–114).
- ☐ Complete *Cuaderno* pages 113, 114, and 115 (L1A pp. 115–117).
  OR
  Complete *Cuaderno para hispanohablantes* pages 112, 113, 114, and 115 (L1A pp. 114–117).
- ☐ Complete *Cuaderno* pages 116, 117, and 118 (L1A pp. 118–120).
  OR
  Complete *Cuaderno para hispanohablantes* pages 116, 117, and 118 (L1A pp. 118–120).
- ☐ Complete *Cuaderno* pages 119, 120, and 121 (L1A pp. 121–123).
  OR
  Complete *Cuaderno para hispanohablantes* pages 119, 120, and 121 (L1A pp. 121–123).

If You Don't Understand . . .

- ☐ For activities that require the CD, listen to the CD in a quiet place. If you get lost, stop the CD and go back.
- ☐ Review the activity directions and study the model. Try to follow the model in your own answers.
- ☐ Say what you want to write before you write it.
- ☐ Write down any questions you have for your teacher.
- ☐ After you write a sentence, check to make sure that it says what you wanted to say.

Absent Student Copymasters

Presentación / Práctica de vocabulario

Materials Checklist

☐ Student text

☐ DVD 1

☐ Video activities copymasters

☐ TXT CD 3 tracks 12–13

☐ *Cuaderno* pages 122–124 (L1A pp. 124–126)

☐ *Cuaderno para hispanohablantes* pages 122–125 (L1A pp. 124–127)

☐ Did You Get It? Copymasters pages 12 and 13

Steps to Follow

☐ Study the vocabulary of **Presentación de vocabulario** (L1 pp. 164–165, L1A pp. 184–186) by reading the words above the photos and the accompanying text. Watch the Vocabulary DVD for **Unidad 3**, **Lección 2** carefully. After watching the DVD, complete the video activities copymasters.

☐ Practice the words of the **Más vocabulario** box on page 165 (L1A p. 186). Read the words aloud. Write the words in your notebook.

☐ Listen to the CD as you read the new vocabulary words. Repeat the words aloud.

☐ Do the **Práctica de vocabulario** (L1 p. 166, LIA p. 187). Complete **Actividades 1** and **2**.

☐ Complete *Cuaderno* pages 122, 123, and 124 (L1A pp. 124–126).
OR
Complete *Cuaderno para hispanohablantes* pages 122, 123, 124, and 125 (L1A pp. 124–127).

☐ Complete the **Para y piensa** box on page 166 (L1A p. 187).

☐ Complete the Did You Get It? Copymasters, pages 12 and 13.

If You Don't Understand . . .

☐ Watch the DVD and listen to the CD in a quiet place. If you get lost, stop and go back.

☐ Read the model before starting so you know what to do. Follow the model.

☐ Read aloud everything that you write. Be sure that you understand what you are reading.

☐ If you have any questions, write them down so you can ask your teacher later.

☐ If the activity has parts for two people, practice both parts.

Absent Student Copymasters

UNIDAD 3 Lección 2

Absent Student Copymasters

Vocabulario en contexto

Materials Checklist

- [ ] Student text
- [ ] DVD 1
- [ ] Video activities copymasters
- [ ] TXT CD 3 track 14
- [ ] Did You Get It? Copymasters pages 12, 14, and 22

Steps to Follow

- [ ] Analyze the photo and read the caption on page 167 (L1A p. 188).
- [ ] Read **Cuando lees** and **Cuando escuchas** under *Strategies* (L1 p. 167, L1A p. 188). Copy the questions.
- [ ] Answer the questions in **Cuando lees** before watching the video.
- [ ] Watch the **Unidad 3**, **Lección 2 Telehistoria escena 1** without your book. Then watch the DVD again and complete the video activities copymasters.
- [ ] Look at the dialogue in the book. Follow along in the book as you watch and listen to the DVD. Use the pictures and context to help you understand the dialogue.
- [ ] Read the **También se dice** box.
- [ ] Complete **Actividades 3** and **4** (L1 p. 168, L1A p. 189).
- [ ] Complete the **Para y piensa** box on page 168 (L1A p. 189).
- [ ] Complete the Did You Get It? Copymasters, pages 12, 14, and 22.

If You Don't Understand . . .

- [ ] Watch the DVD and listen to the CD in a quiet place. If you get lost, stop and go back.
- [ ] Write out the directions in your own words.
- [ ] Read the model before starting so you know what to do. Follow the model.
- [ ] Read aloud everything that you write. Be sure that you understand what you are reading.
- [ ] If you have any questions, write them down so you can ask your teacher later.
- [ ] Think about what you are trying to say when you write a sentence. After you write your sentence, check to make sure that it says what you wanted to say.

Absent Student Copymasters

Presentación / Práctica de gramática

Materials Checklist

☐ Student text

☐ *Cuaderno* pages 125–127 (L1A pp. 127–129)

☐ *Cuaderno para hispanohablantes* pages 126–128 (L1A pp. 128–130)

☐ TXT CD 3 track 16

☐ Did You Get It? Copymasters pages 15, 16, and 23

☐ ClassZone.com

Steps to Follow

☐ Study possessive adjectives (L1 p. 169, L1A p. 190).

☐ Complete **Actividades 5, 6, 7,** and **8** (L1 pp. 170–171).

☐ Complete **Actividades 5, 6, 7, 8,** and **9** (L1A pp. 191–193).

☐ Complete *Cuaderno* pages 125, 126, and 127 (L1A pages 127, 128, and 129).
OR
Complete *Cuaderno para hispanohablantes* pages 126, 127, and 128 (L1A pages 128, 129, and 130).

☐ Complete the **Para y piensa** box on page 171 (L1A p. 193).

☐ Complete the Did You Get It? Copymasters, pages 15, 16, and 23.

If You Don't Understand . . .

☐ For activities that require listening, listen to the CD in a quiet place. If you get lost, stop the CD and go back.

☐ Re-read the directions for the activity you find difficult. Write out the directions in your own words.

☐ Read the model a few times so you are certain that you understand what to do.

☐ Read aloud everything that you write.

☐ If the activity has parts for two people, practice both parts.

☐ Think about what you are trying to say when you write a sentence. After you write your sentence, check to make sure that it says what you wanted to say.

☐ Use the Animated Grammar to help you understand.

☐ Use the Leveled Grammar Practice on the @Home Tutor.

Absent Student Copymasters

UNIDAD 3 Lección 2

Absent Student Copymasters

Gramática en contexto

Materials Checklist

- [ ] Student text
- [ ] TXT DVD 1
- [ ] Video activities copymasters
- [ ] TXT CD 3 track 15
- [ ] Did You Get It? Copymasters pages 15 and 17

Steps to Follow

- [ ] Look at the photo on page 172 (L1A p. 194). What do you think is happening?
- [ ] Read **Cuando lees** and **Cuando escuchas** under *Strategies* (L1 p. 172, L1A p. 194). Copy the questions.
- [ ] Watch the **Unidad 3, Lección 2 Telehistoria escena 2** without your book. Then watch the CD again and complete the video activities copymaster.
- [ ] Look at the dialogue in the book. Follow along in the book as you listen to the CD. Use the pictures and context to help you understand the dialogue.
- [ ] Complete **Actividades 9**, **10**, and **11** (L1 p. 173).
- [ ] Complete **Actividades 10**, **11**, and **12** (L1A p. 195).
- [ ] Complete the **Para y piensa** box on page 173 (L1A p. 195).
- [ ] Complete the Did You Get It? Copymasters, pages 15 and 17.

If You Don't Understand . . .

- [ ] Go to a quiet place and watch the DVD. If you become confused, replay the section that was confusing.
- [ ] Listen to the CD in a quiet place. If you get lost, stop the CD and go back.
- [ ] Re-read the directions for the activity you find difficult. Write out the directions in your own words.
- [ ] Read the model a few times so you are certain that you understand what to do. Follow the model.
- [ ] If you have any questions, write them down for your teacher to answer later.
- [ ] If the activity has parts for two people, do both parts of the activity.

Absent Student Copymasters

Presentación / Práctica de gramática

Materials Checklist

☐ Student text

☐ *Cuaderno* pages 128–130 (L1A pp. 130–132)

☐ *Cuaderno para hispanohablantes* pages 129–132 (L1A pp. 131–134)

☐ TXT CD 3 tracks 16–17

☐ Did You Get It? Copymasters pages 18 and 19

Steps to Follow

☐ Read about comparatives on page 174 (L1A p. 196).

☐ Complete **Actividades 12** and **13** (L1 p. 175).

☐ Complete **Actividades 13, 14, 15,** and **16** (L1A pp. 197–198).

☐ Listen to TXT CD 3 track 16 as you follow along in the **Pronunciación** activity on p. 175 (L1A p. 191).

☐ Complete **Actividad 14** (L1 p. 176).

☐ Complete **Actividades 17** and **18** (L1A p. 199).

☐ Complete *Cuaderno* pages 128, 129, and 130 (L1A pp. 130–132).
OR
Complete *Cuaderno para hispanohablantes* pages 129, 130, 131, and 132 (L1A pp. 131–134).

☐ Complete the **Para y piensa** box on page 176 (L1A p. 199).

☐ Complete the Did You Get It? Copymasters, pages 18 and 19.

If You Don't Understand . . .

☐ For activities that require listening, listen to the CD in a quiet place. If you get lost, stop the CD and go back.

☐ Re-read the directions for the activity you find difficult. Write out the directions in your own words.

☐ Read the model a few times so you are certain that you understand what to do.

☐ Read aloud everything that you write. Be sure that you understand what you are reading.

☐ If you have any questions, write them down for your teacher.

☐ If the activity has parts for two people, practice both parts.

Absent Student Copymasters

Todo junto

Materials Checklist

- [ ] Student text
- [ ] DVD 1
- [ ] Video activities copymasters
- [ ] *Cuaderno* pages 131–132 (L1A pp. 133–134)
- [ ] *Cuaderno para hispanohablantes* pages 133–134 (L1A pp. 135–136)
- [ ] Did You Get It? Copymasters pages 18 and 20
- [ ] WB CD 2 tracks 11–14
- [ ] HL CD 1 tracks 21–24
- [ ] TXT CD 3 tracks 18–20

Steps to Follow

- [ ] Look at the photos on page 177 (L1A p. 200). What do you think is happening?
- [ ] Read **Cuando lees** and **Cuando escuchas** under *Strategies* (L1 p. 177, L1A p. 200). Copy the questions.
- [ ] Review the content of **Unidad 3**, **Telehistoria escena 1** and **escena 2**.
- [ ] Read the script and try to understand the dialogue based on the picture. Complete **Cuando lees**.
- [ ] Watch the **Unidad 3, Lección 2 Telehistoria escena 3** without your book. Then watch the DVD again and complete the video activities copymaster.
- [ ] Complete **Actividades 16, 17, 18, 19**, and **20** (L1 pp. 178–179).
- [ ] Complete **Actividades 19, 20, 21, 22**, and **23** (L1A p. 201–202).
- [ ] Complete *Cuaderno* pages 131 and 132 (L1A pp. 133–134).
  OR
  Complete *Cuaderno para hispanohablantes* pages 133 and 134 (L1A pp. 135–136).
- [ ] Complete the Did You Get It? Copymasters, pages 18 and 20.

If You Don't Understand . . .

- [ ] Read the model a few times so you are certain that you understand what to do. Follow the model.
- [ ] If the activity has parts for two people, practice both parts.

Absent Student Copymasters

Lectura cultural

Materials Checklist

☐ Student text

☐ TXT CD 3 track 21

Steps to Follow

☐ Read **Strategy: Leer** (L1 p. 180, L1A p. 204).

☐ Read **La quinceañera** on pages 180 and 181 (L1A pp. 204–205).

☐ Look at the photos that accompany the text.

☐ Follow along with the text on TXT CD 3 track 21.

☐ Check your comprehension by completing the **¿Comprendiste?** and **¿Y tú?** sections of **Para y piensa** on page 181 (L1A p. 205).

If You Don't Understand . . .

☐ Listen to the CD in a quiet place. If you get lost, stop the CD and go back.

☐ Re-read the directions for the activity you find difficult. Write out the directions in your own words.

☐ Read aloud everything that you write. Be sure that you understand what you are reading.

☐ If you have any questions, write them down so you can ask your teacher later.

☐ If the activity has parts for two people, complete both parts.

☐ Think about what you are trying to say when you write a sentence. After you write your sentence, check to make sure that it says what you wanted to say.

Absent Student Copymasters

Proyectos culturales

Materials Checklist

☐ Student text

Steps to Follow

☐ Read **Instrumentos de Puerto Rico y Perú** (L1 p. 182, L1A p. 206).

☐ Make your own rhythm pattern in **Proyecto 1**.

☐ Try to create your own **zampoña** in **Proyecto 2**.

☐ Complete **En tu comunidad** on page 182 (L1A p. 206).

If You Don't Understand . . .

☐ Re-read the directions for the activity you find difficult. Write the directions in your own words.

☐ If you have any questions, write them down so you can ask your teacher later.

Absent Student Copymasters

Repaso de la lección

Materials Checklist

- ☐ Student text
- ☐ *Cuaderno* pages 133–144 (L1A pp. 135–146)
- ☐ *Cuaderno para hispanohablantes* pages 135–144 (L1A pp. 137–146)
- ☐ WB CD 2 tracks 15–20
- ☐ TXT CD 3 track 22

Steps to Follow

- ☐ Read the bullet points under **¡Llegada!** on page 184 (L1A p. 208).
- ☐ Complete **Actividades 1**, **2**, **3**, **4**, and **5** (L1 pp. 184–185, L1A pp. 208–209).
- ☐ Complete *Cuaderno* pages 133, 134, and 135 (L1A pp. 135–137).
- ☐ Complete *Cuaderno* pages 136, 137, and 138 (L1A pp. 138–140).
  OR
  Complete *Cuaderno para hispanohablantes* pages 135, 136, 137, and 138
  (L1A pp. 137–140).
- ☐ Complete *Cuaderno* pages 139, 140, and 141 (L1A pp. 141–143).
  OR
  Complete *Cuaderno para hispanohablantes* pages 139, 140, and 141
  (L1A pp. 141–143).
- ☐ Complete *Cuaderno* pages 142, 143, and 144 (L1A pp. 144–146).
  OR
  Complete *Cuaderno para hispanohablantes* pages 142, 143, and 144
  (L1A pp. 144–146).

If You Don't Understand . . .

- ☐ If you are having trouble with an activity, complete the items you can do first.
- ☐ For activities that require the CD, listen to the CD in a quiet place. If you get lost, stop the CD and go back.

Absent Student Copymasters

Comparación cultural

Materials Checklist

☐ Student text

☐ TXT CD 3 track 23

Steps to Follow

☐ Look at the photos and read the text of **¿Qué comemos?** on pages 186 and 187 (L1A pp. 210–211).

☐ Follow steps 1 and 2 under **Strategy: Escribir**.

☐ Complete **Compara con tu mundo** on page 186 (L1A p. 210).

If You Don't Understand . . .

☐ Make sure you are in an area where you can concentrate.

☐ Listen to the CD as many times as necessary.

☐ Re-read the directions for the activity you find difficult. Write the directions in your own words.

☐ Read everything aloud. Be sure that you understand what you are reading.

☐ Write down any questions you have for your teacher.

☐ Think about what you are trying to say when you write a sentence. After you write your sentence, check to make sure that it says what you wanted to say.

Absent Student Copymasters

Repaso inclusivo

Materials Checklist

- ☐ Student text
- ☐ TXT CD 3 track 24

Steps to Follow

- ☐ Go over the options for review, **Actividades 1**, **2**, **3**, **4**, **5**, **6**, and **7** (pp. 188–189).
- ☐ Go over the options for review, **Actividades 1**, **2**, **3**, **4**, **5**, and **6** (L1A pp. 212–213).
- ☐ Listen to TXT CD 3 track 24 for **Actividad 1** on page 188 (L1A p. 212). Answer the questions.
- ☐ Present another person for **Actividad 2** on page 188 (L1A p. 212).
- ☐ Plan a family reunion for **Actividad 4** on page 188 (L1A p. 213).
- ☐ Complete **Actividad 7** on page 189.

If You Don't Understand . . .

- ☐ Listen to the CD as many times as you need to complete **Actividad 1**.
- ☐ Re-read the directions for the activity you find difficult. Write out the directions in your own words.
- ☐ Say what you want to write before you write it.
- ☐ If you have any questions, write them down so you can ask your teacher later.
- ☐ Practice both parts of any partner activities.
- ☐ After you write a sentence, check to make sure that it says what you wanted to say.